THE FIRST-TIME LANDLORD

A New Landlord's Guide
to Surviving (and Maybe Thriving)

LISA BENTLEY

ISBN: 978-1-7399419-4-9

Written by Lisa Bentley.
Illustrations created by the author with the assistance of AI tools.
Published by Look Inside Smile Again, United Kingdom.

Exclusion of Liability and Disclaimer

This book is a work of non-fiction based on the author's personal experiences as a landlord. In a small number of cases, names, locations, or identifying details may have been changed to protect the privacy of others.

While every effort has been made to ensure the information in this book is accurate at the time of writing, it is provided for general guidance only. Laws, regulations, and best practices can change, and it is impossible to anticipate every circumstance in which the information may be used. The advice shared reflects the author's own experience and should not be relied upon as a substitute for professional, legal, or financial advice.

To the fullest extent permitted by law, the author, publisher, and any associated parties disclaim any liability for loss or damage arising directly or indirectly from the use or misuse of the information contained in this book. Readers are encouraged to check official government guidance or seek professional advice where appropriate.

A CIP catalogue record for this book is available from The British Library.

www.lisabentley.co.uk

In Loving Memory of

Mark Bentley

1973-2006

What might have been, if we had known.

Contents

Dear Reader

This isn't your typical 'get-rich-quick' landlord guide. I didn't write it to sell a scheme or preach from a distance. I wrote it from the heart, drawing on more than 20 years of real-life experience – the wins, the mistakes, and the lessons learned the hard way.

Initially, I created this book for my two sons. I wanted them to have everything I've discovered in one place, should they ever need it. Along the way, I realised these stories, tips and warnings could help others too, whether you became a landlord by choice, by chance, or by inheritance.

Inside, you'll find practical advice, cautionary tales, and a little humour. Take what serves you, leave what doesn't, and most importantly, trust yourself to make informed decisions.

If this book saves you stress, money, or even just a single sleepless night, then it's done its job.

With honesty and experience,

Lisa

Introduction

So, you've decided – or accidentally become – a landlord. How are you feeling? Daunted? Excited? A bit of both? Either way, congratulations. Because owning a rental property isn't just about collecting rent and sipping tea while tenants do all the work (though that would be nice and my goodness I do love a cup of Twinings). Instead, it's a mix of detective work, social psychology, DIY skills, and some days being a landlord is a better workout than anything my local gym could dream up.

However you ended up in this world of tenants, taps, and tax returns, let me reassure you: those mixed feelings – the flutter of excitement and the stab of fear – are perfectly normal.

When my husband, Mark, and I bought our first property back in 2004, Mark thought we'd cracked the code. He would retire from his stressful job in London 10 years later and we'd live the rest of our lives with freedom, peace and joy.

Estate agents made it sound so simple:

> "Just let it out and watch the rent roll in!"
> "It basically pays for itself!"
> "Property always goes up!"
> "Passive income!"

Yeah. About that.

Why this book exists

I never set out to be a landlord nor to write a guide for others who find themselves in this role. But life rarely follows a single formula. Back in December 2006, after the sudden and tragic loss of my husband, I was left with two young boys to raise, but also with two buy-to-let properties I had little choice but to manage.

And the truth is, I wasn't ever excited about becoming a landlord. Even when my husband was alive. Back then, I'd heard too many horror stories. The properties had been my husband's dream – not mine – but I agreed as it was a way to create a future home and income for our two boys. When my husband passed, the timing couldn't have been worse: I was a full-time mum, we were due to complete on our second rental property the day he died, and our life insurance papers were still sitting on the sideboard waiting to be posted. To compound matters, my precious five-year-old was born with a genetic condition, which meant regular hospital appointments, my two-year-old clung constantly to my hip, and all the while I was in the second year of studying for a degree in Psychology with The Open University. Managing rental properties was the last thing I wanted to take on. Yet, I felt I had no choice. For the sake of stability and for my sons' well-being, I had to step up and carry forward what my husband had started and dreamed of for all of us. Continuing with the property game felt like a way to keep his dreams alive through me, and that mattered enormously.

As the next few years went by and my boys grew older, I grew stronger too. Then one day, a house just two doors down from one of my rentals came up for sale, and I couldn't resist. I had this slightly romantic notion of my children living close to one another when they were older, especially with my eldest having a hearing impairment. If there were intruders or an emergency, they'd have each other. That motherly instinct to keep them safe, and the quiet certainty that Mark would have felt the same, became my driving force. Then, with that house in play, another house came up. I was driving around the neighbourhood when I saw the For Sale sign and thought to myself, 'It's too good an opportunity not to view it.' This happened again and then again. But still, there was a constant other worry that weighed heavily on me and kept me awake at night: What if something happened to me? Sure, my sons would inherit these properties, but would they know how to manage them once they grew up? Would they be taken advantage of, or even sell them out of fear or frustration? Would they feel an immense amount of stress and anxiety if they kept them, and guilt if they sold them? I believe action is the antidote to fear, and so to prepare them and give myself a restful night's sleep, I began making notes, writing down what I'd learned, the pitfalls to avoid, and the truths some letting agents never told me.

Those notes I made over the years grew into this book. Originally intended as a 'Mum's Guide to Renting' guidebook for my sons, I realised along the way that my knowledge could help others too – especially the 'accidental landlords' who find themselves in this position unexpectedly. Because here's the truth: not everyone chooses to be a landlord. And when you don't, it's all too easy to be overwhelmed, misled or even exploited.

So here we are.

Who this book is for

This book is for:

- First-time landlords.
- Accidental landlords (the "I didn't ask for this" crowd).

- Tired, jaded landlords.
- Any landlord with one or more single let properties (not HMOs) in England who wants to avoid costly mistakes.

If that's you, you're in the right place.

I hope that what follows will offer both practical guidance and reassurance that you are not alone.

Why listen to me?

I've been in property for over 20 years, and some of my knowledge is built on the shoulders of those before me – my late husband's parents, for one. My eldest son, now 25 years old, with a Master's in Business and real estate experience, has recently added his own wisdom to the pile. Along the way, I've swapped stories with landlords from all walks of life, from seasoned pros to people just figuring it out one leaky tap at a time.

Here's what I am not:

- I’m not an estate or letting agent.
- I’m not a mortgage advisor.
- I’m not a glossy ‘guru’.

I’m simply a woman in her mid-fifties who was thrown into this world without a map and learned the hard way. What you’ll find here isn’t a sugar-coated fantasy about passive income. It’s an honest, hopeful and practical guide to surviving – and maybe thriving – as a landlord.

What this book is not

I will never give you mortgage advice – I’m not qualified nor willing. The same applies to personal ownership vs. setting up a limited company.

What this is *is* a candid, sometimes funny, sometimes sobering look at landlording: the things agents gloss over, the traps you can avoid, and the small wins that make a big difference.

And rest assured, you don't need to get everything right – you just need to be one step ahead.

What you'll learn in this book

By the end of this book, you'll know how to:

- Handle tenants with confidence – from finding them, to keeping them happy, to managing issues fairly.
- Protect yourself legally and financially – so you don't get caught out by hidden costs, dodgy advice, or fine print.
- Manage property problems without panic – from the everyday niggles to the 3 am emergencies.
- Think like a business owner – because whether you planned to or not, you're now running a small business.
- Avoid costly mistakes – the kind I made early on, so you don't have to.

- Find the balance – between protecting your investment and remembering this isn't just bricks and mortar, it's somebody's home.

> This isn't about being perfect. It's about being prepared, staying calm and learning to make property work for you, instead of the other way around.

How to use this book

This book is designed to be your companion through the ups, downs and downright bizarre moments of being a landlord. Think of it as part practical guide, part diary and part 'survival manual'. Here's how to get the most out of it.

1. Read in order... or jump around

- The chapters are organised to follow the landlord journey, from the start of letting a property in the UK to ongoing management and finances.

- You can read straight through or skip to the sections most relevant to you – finding a tenant, dealing with emergencies or tenant tips, for example.

2. Use the case studies & tips

- Real-life and horror tales illustrate key points and help you spot pitfalls before they happen.
- TLDR (Too Long Didn't Read) sections summarise the essentials for quick reference.

3. Forms & Templates

At the back of the book, there's space for you to store your own:

- Contact details for contractors, agents and tenants.
- Key dates for certificates, inspections and renewals.

- Notes from property visits or tenant interactions.
- Templates for welcome letters, inspection checklists and maintenance logs.

4. **Make it your own**

- Use the margins, post-it notes, or the dedicated pages at the back of this book, to jot reminders, observations or plans.
- The more you personalise it, the more it becomes a tool for your sanity and organisation.

5. **Refer back often**

- Landlord rules change, emergencies happen, and tenants are unpredictable.
- Keep this book handy for reference. It's your 'cheat sheet' for quick solutions, reminders and inspiration.

Read, refer, record, and reuse. Treat this book as a mix of handbook, diary, and a safety net. It will save you time, money and sleepless nights.

A final thought before we begin

You're about to start a journey that's part business, part life school.

It can be frustrating, rewarding, occasionally absurd, and often nothing like what you imagined. But, like most things in life, if you approach it with a steady head and a willingness to learn, you can make it work – maybe even thrive.

So buckle up. The doors are about to open.

A Gentle Reminder:

This is your property, but it will also be someone else's home.

Key Takeaway

Being a landlord isn't a ticket to free money. It's not about power or ego either. It's about responsibility, patience and people. You'll make mistakes along the way – we all do – but each one teaches you something valuable. This role will humble you at times and test your limits at others, yet also bring moments of real pride and purpose. Approach it with empathy, integrity and a genuine desire to do things right. Then you won't just build properties – you'll build trust, resilience and a legacy you can feel proud of.

CHAPTER 1

Getting the House Fit for Rent

So, you've got your first buy-to-let. Huge congratulations. Whether this was a carefully planned decision or something you somehow stumbled into, you did it. You're officially a landlord!

How's it all feeling now? A mix of excitement, mild panic, and the occasional, "What on earth have I done?" moment? If so, that's perfectly normal. Whether you've inherited a property (or a few), taken a leap of faith, or are a seasoned landlord who's just plain exhausted, welcome to the club. Every landlord, new or experienced, knows that strange blend of thrill and terror bubbling beneath the surface. I'll never forget the night I stayed up until 2 am Googling, 'What counts as wear and tear,' convinced I was about to make a huge mistake with my first tenant. Another time, I stayed awake all night whispering quiet prayers that the roof survives one more winter. So please don't worry, you're in good company.

The first 30 days after getting the keys

Assuming your property doesn't need a licence from your local authority (this is area-based; check with your local council if you are unsure), before you even think about tenants, you need to take time to get your property properly set up. These first few weeks are about laying solid foundations: safety, compliance, and smart organisation. Do it right now, and you'll save yourself endless headaches, sleepless nights and potential legal tangles later. Trust me, it's easier (and cheaper) to do things properly upfront.

1. Buildings Insurance

First things first, make sure your buy-to-let buildings insurance is in place. And yes, as dull as it sounds, please do read the small print.

Policy costs can vary depending on who's living in the property, and if it becomes vacant, you must inform your insurer. Most policies allow around 60 days of no occupancy, but don't assume – check. After a certain period, terms often change, sometimes with higher premiums or specific conditions (like turning off and draining down the water system).

When it comes to cost, remember it's based on the **rebuild value**, not the market value of the property. Insurers will usually calculate this for you, but you can sense-check it via the Association of British Insurers website.

And if your property is leasehold, be sure to check exactly what's covered in the freeholder's insurance – and just as importantly, what isn't.

In terms of contents insurance, unless you're renting your property furnished, this is your tenant's responsibility, not yours. You could remind them of this when they eventually move in.

Be sure to file any paperwork somewhere safe and keep a note of the cost for tax return purposes.

2. Organisation

Secondly, please go and buy yourself an **annual diary**. The good old-fashioned paper kind (sorry trees). Nothing fancy is needed. Keep it somewhere visible with a pen nearby, because trust me, you'll use it more than you expect. We all like to think we'll remember things, but that sticky note on the fridge has a sneaky habit of vanishing just when you need it most. And there's always the fear of your phone breaking or, worse still, being stolen.

Of course, you can manage everything digitally if that suits you – spreadsheets, apps, and automated reminders all have their place. But I still recommend keeping a physical paper trail. For me, there's something reassuring about knowing that, if anything ever happens to me, my sons can find everything easily. No passwords, no searching through endless files. Just a clear record of what matters. It's not just about staying organised; it's about responsibility, legacy, and peace of mind. On that note, however, I have recently created an email address specifically for my properties. I have found this really useful to easily access online documents when necessary.

A boxed binder is useful too, or a ring binder with plastic sleeves, so you can store hard copies of receipts and keys. For me, I rest easy with a paper trail for those "Just in case I can't remember where I filed it" online moments.

Make it a non-negotiable to jot down key dates, like when your gas safety certificate or insurance renewal is due, and set a reminder a few weeks beforehand in your diary, leaving it in a place you'll easily notice and think to check. **Note:** Your gas safety check can be carried out up to two months before its expiry date without affecting the original renewal date.

3. Keys

If you haven't got them already, I would recommend getting yourself two extra sets of front and back door keys cut. Keep the receipt and make a note of the mileage to and from the key cutters, as you can offset the cost and mileage on your tax return. It's not wasted money as you'll need the extra keys for your tenant, and if there's more than one tenant, you'll leave two sets with them. And, in the meantime, you can safely leave a set with your letting agent or trusted friend, builder, or anyone helping you out without compromising your own access to the property. Builders can easily lose keys, so be sure to label them (with your name, not address) before handing them over. I would recommend the same when dealing with letting agents, just to be on the safe side.

4. Meters, Readings, and Photo Evidence

Next up is the task of locating your **gas, electricity, and water meters**. Take readings before anyone moves in. Write them down *and* photograph them; timestamped photos are landlord gold if a dispute ever crops up.

If you're unsure where they are:

- **Gas cupboard:** This is often outside, and you may need a **triangular key** to open its door (you can purchase these online if the previous owner didn't leave one). Personally, I think it's a good idea to have one for yourself as well, if you don't have one at home. Speaking from experience, you don't want them damaging the cupboard trying to open it without a key.

- **Water meter:** This is usually in the pavement in front of the house, and check that the **serial number** on the meter matches your account. Sometimes there is more than one meter nearby and, from personal experience, it's easy to get them mixed up.

- **Electricity meter:** This is sometimes located outside, but usually under the stairs or in a hallway cupboard.

Pro Tip:

Create a "Utilities Info" sheet for tenants. Note down meter locations, suppliers, and any access details. It saves everyone a dozen phone calls or texts later.

5. Safety first

Make sure there's a **working smoke alarm on each floor** and a **carbon monoxide alarm** near any fuel-burning appliance. This is a legal requirement. Test them and, for peace of mind, video yourself testing it. You'll thank yourself later when someone swears, "It never worked." **Note:** Always check again on the morning of the tenant(s) move in date.

If any alarms are missing, replace them before listing the property. Secure them properly too; loose alarms have a strange tendency to 'wander off' between tenancies. Especially the carbon monoxide alarms.

It is also important to mention your requirement to assess the risk of exposure to Legionella:

Legionella Safety Checklist

- Identify all water systems, especially rarely used taps, showers, tanks, and pipework.
- Keep hot water ≥60°C (stored) / ≥50°C (delivered); cold water ≤20°C.
- Flush unused outlets 1–2 minutes weekly.
- Clean showerheads and hoses regularly.
- Avoid stagnant sections of pipework.
- Keep a simple log of checks, flushing, and cleaning.
- Arrange professional testing only if risk is identified.

6. Certificates, Councils & Compliance

Whether or not your property was previously rented, it's vital you check that these are up to date:

- ☐ **Smoke Alarms & Carbon Monoxide Alarm:** As previously mentioned, smoke alarms should be fitted one per floor, and the carbon monoxide alarm should be placed near gas or solid-fuel appliances. Your gas engineer will advise you, and please ensure the carbon monoxide detector is mounted on the wall to prevent it from being moved or lost.

- ☐ **Gas Safety Certificate:** This is required annually.

- ☐ **EICR:** This is an Electrical Installation Condition Report, required every 5 years. Electricians get booked up, so schedule fast, at least 2 weeks ahead.

- ☐ **EPC:** This is your Energy Performance Certificate, and it is required whenever a property is newly marketed for rent or sale. It is valid for 10 years, and since April 2020, unless an exemption is registered, all rental properties must have an EPC rating of E or above. However, by 2030, rental properties may need an EPC C rating, and the new Decent Homes Standard could follow. Therefore, expect some extra costs to stay legal, safe, and lettable.

My advice is to check the latest regulations online or ask your letting agent, as regulations may have changed after publishing this book.

Please note: I saved £40 using a local EPC assessor instead of going through a letting agency – they charge commission on top.

- ☐ **Right to Rent:** Check tenant identity and eligibility. If you are using a letting agency, they will do that for you as part of their service.

- ☐ **Deposit Protection:** Must be in a government-approved scheme. See Chapters 2 and 4 for more details.

- ☐ **Landlord Insurance:** Essential, but don't claim for every drip, or next year's premium will bite.

- ☐ **Chimney Sweep:** An annual certificate is required for insurance validity. If the chimney is to be unused, block it off, tell the tenants and note it in the tenancy agreement.

- ☐ **Boiler service:** Annual check recommended. My plumber does mine at the same time as the gas safety certificate.

- ☐ Be sure to notify your **council tax office** when the property becomes empty or changes occupancy. Sadly, the days of free 'vacancy periods' are over.

Note:

Don't forget, you can always change energy suppliers (look for one with no exit fee) if the current supplier's charges are higher than those of other companies. Always give your home address as your correspondence address so that bills don't go astray.

Top Tip:

Diarise expiry dates and avoid relying on tenants to check them. Record the dates and set a reminder a couple of weeks earlier – better safe than sorry.

To the Future Landlord:

There is no official date at the time of publishing this book, but please be aware that the Renters' Rights Act will introduce a Private Rented Sector Landlord Ombudsman, which all private landlords in England must join – including those using a managing agent. The government will also set up a landlord database. According to the latest reports, local councils can enforce compliance with civil penalties of up to £7,000 for first-time breaches and up to £40,000 or criminal prosecution for repeated offences. Tenants may also apply for rent repayment orders if a landlord persistently fails to join.

7. The Snag List: Your Pre-Tenant Detective Work

i. **Do a full walk-around before your builder is enlisted or anyone moves in.** Check taps, locks, windows, lights, and appliances. And don't forget the loft. Look for leaks, mouse droppings, or anything suspicious. Make notes, snap photos, even take a short video. This is your baseline for future inspections and your proof if anything breaks later.

ii. **Check your stopcock... properly.** Tiny valves can be lifesavers or disaster-makers. **Case in point**: I never thought to check my stop cock worked, nor did I think to keep my heating on low when I went on holiday with my extended family in the thick of winter. To cut a long story short, I came home to heavily settled snow, plus a burst pipe in the loft. I remember opening the front door to see water pouring through my ceiling. I tried the stopcock under the sink, but it didn't work and finding the one in the road, underneath the snow and ice, was an absolute nightmare.

Lesson: Locate your stopcock, turn it on and off, and make sure it actually works. Show your future tenant where it is. This tiny check can save you (and your tenant) from a soaking disaster and a lengthy, stressful insurance claim.

iii. **The Reality Check: Why preparation matters.** This is where many new landlords can trip up, underestimating how long it takes to get a property truly 'tenant-ready'.

Here's what other landlords and I have learnt over the years:

- **Timelines lie.** The initial advert to move in can easily take a month or more. As well, not all builders work to your time frame; sometimes the job takes longer than anticipated, unexpected problems, or another urgent job may come up that they have to attend to. I have a good, trustworthy builder; he has come to my rescue in the past, putting another job for another customer on hold for me, so I totally respect him if he has to dash off for another landlord's emergency. Compassion and patience help. Have a contingency fund just in case.

- **Tenant notice periods** mean people can't move instantly, as most need to give at least four weeks' notice to their current landlord. And if they don't, question why. Investigate and don't be too shy to ask. I think it's wise to know as much as you can about the person potentially living in your property; there's more about that in Chapter 3.

- **Advertise early.** Contact a letting agency or agencies (if you are planning on using one) once the property is clean and functional, not perfect. You can always make contact as soon as you hold the keys, and be guided by when they think it best to start advertising. They may have people on their books they can pre-warn.

- **Quick wins:** Fresh hallway paint, clean carpets, new bulbs, sparkling and serviceable kitchens and bathrooms. These days, showers matter.

- **White goods** aren't necessary; it's best that the tenant provides their own. It saves you money and time cleaning them when they leave. It could be that you inform the tenant (and ensure it is written in the tenancy agreement) that they may use the white goods currently in situ (if there are any), but it would be down to them to purchase new ones if they break down, or they wish to replace them. Ensure any portable electrical appliances that plug in and can be moved are PAT tested.

- **Curtains and blinds:** Not essential; however, any blinds must comply with safety standards. The same applies to furniture and furnishings, which must meet fire and safety regulations.

Pro Tip:

Small Things That Make a Big Difference

Provide a chopping board: A small pearl of wisdom I picked up along the way. It doesn't have to be anything fancy, but having one in place helps protect your worktops from scratches and stains. Not every tenant thinks of buying one straight away, so it's a simple, thoughtful touch that's often appreciated – and can help avoid unnecessary wear-and-tear disputes later on.

Provide front and back door mats: Unfortunately, not all tenants (and visitors) take their shoes off. Mats act as a subtle reminder to wipe feet before entering, keeping your floors cleaner and reducing maintenance.

The decorating debate

You might ask yourself, "How perfect should your property look?" With over 20 years of experience, here's my honest answer:

- Stick to **neutral colours**. Magnolia may be 'landlord beige', but it's easy to touch up.
- Avoid brilliant white as fingerprints multiply overnight. Use washable paint rather than the quick dry.
- Forget 'Soft Whisper of Moonlight' cream, as you'll *never* find the same shade again. Or remember what colour you chose.
- Professional decorators give you a flawless finish (and less stress, but unless you are closely connected to one, they come at a cost). DIY can be perfectly fine once the tenant's furniture is in. I guess it boils down to your time and budget. The sooner a house is ready, the sooner you can get a tenant, and the sooner you start receiving rent.
- Durability beats design. Remember, you're running a business, not curating an art gallery.

Taxes and records

Being a landlord means being a business owner. HMRC doesn't care whether it's by accident or otherwise. Please keep meticulous records:

- Rent, repairs, certificates, mileage, receipts. Remember, even small items add up.
- File annual (and possibly quarterly, depending on your income) tax returns. More about this can be found in Chapter 5.

Note: With the government making tax digital, ensure you comply with the rules. I currently use Xero, and another landlord friend of mine trusts his spreadsheet. The choice is yours – or your accountant's – but will also depend upon your income threshold. Without doubt, a good accountant is worth their weight in gold. And fewer panic attacks.

Real life surprises *(a few of mine)*

- A dishwasher that broke two weeks after handover. Be mindful of fitting white goods; it could cost you dearly; doing so isn't compulsory, and quite often tenants have their own anyhow.
- A 'sticky' front door that snapped the key in half.
- A slow leak that turned into a damp cupboard.
- The roof that leaked directly onto the boiler, breaking it in January (of all the seasons, it had to be winter).

Moral: No matter how thorough you are, life happens and tenants will find what you missed. Keep a contingency fund for 'Day Two Disasters'.

My advice

- Being local helps. If you live nearby (or know someone reliable who does), you're already winning.

- Invest in a basic toolkit: multi-bit screwdriver (an electric one is brilliant), tape measure, triangular key, hammer, pliers, adjustable wrench, torch, utility knife, pen, and notepad. An extension lead is useful too. All this can potentially save you time and unnecessary stress.

- If you are able to, visit the house at different times whilst it's unoccupied. You will get to know it better that way. You might assume the outside sensor light is working during the day, but come evening, that might not be the case.

- Always **inform utility companies** yourself when tenants move out and never assume they've done it.

True story: I once got a **court summons** for unpaid council tax, years after a tenant left because the council "never received my update". It was back in the day when Landlords didn't have to pay for the first three months of an unoccupied property. Luckily, I had the original email. No apology, but they dropped the charges instantly.

Lesson: Always get tenancy changeovers in writing.

Budget smartly

Plan ahead for:

- Safety certificates (Gas, EPC, EICR).
- Insurance.
- Maintenance (always more than you think).
- Void periods (no rent doesn't mean no bills; you will be responsible for any utilities and, depending upon your council, council tax at the standard rate).

Properties can be money pits *and* long-term investments.

Manage both with realism.

Quick checklist

- ☐ Buildings insurance updated and vacancy declared if applicable.
- ☐ Gas, electricity, and water readings noted and photographed.
- ☐ Smoke and carbon monoxide alarms tested, recorded, and replaced if needed.
- ☐ Gas Safety and EICR certificates in place.
- ☐ Council tax and utilities informed.
- ☐ Snag list completed and saved for records.

Takeaway:

Preparation and compliance may not be glamorous, but they're your safety net. Get them right, and you'll protect your tenants, your investment, and your sanity. The boring stuff is what makes the business sustainable.

CHAPTER 2

Letting Agents – Friend, Foe or just Expensive Middlemen?

Letting agents often greet you with a smile and a glossy brochure, and some are genuinely helpful (I have a lot of respect for the good ones I work with). Others? Let's just say they could sell sunglasses in a cave.

The truth is, a letting agent can be your greatest ally, your biggest frustration, or simply an expensive middleman. The key is knowing how to work with them without feeling like you're being walked over.

Most operate on a "no find, no fee" basis, so their motivation is clear – they're paid to get someone in. Which is great…as long as it's the *right* someone.

Your four main choices

Costs can vary from one area to another, one agent to another, and often can depend upon whether you live inside or outside London. But when it comes to letting a property, you've got four basic options. Ask yourself, "Which one will help me sleep best at night?"

1. **Fully managed service.**

2. **Tenant-find only.**

3. **Rent Collection Service.**

4. **DIY (Do it yourself).**

Each has pros, cons, and price tags. Let's break them down.

1. Fully managed service

The agent handles everything: advertising, viewings, contracts, deposits, rent collection, repairs, inspections – the lot.

Sounds blissful, right? Except it comes at a hefty monthly percentage of your rent. And 'fully managed' doesn't always mean 'stress-free'.

Even with full management, you **might** still face:

- Unexpected bills you weren't consulted about.
- Higher fees for repairs.
- Vague and/or delayed monthly statements requiring forensic accounting.
- Missed safety checks they swear they booked.
- Potentially a smug "We advised you..." when things go wrong.

Best for: Landlords who live far away, hate admin, or have no time.

Note: Not all letting agents are 'bad'. Some are simply busier than others. Some have targets to meet. Some care more than others.

2. Tenant-find only

The agent advertises the property, takes the holding deposit, vets tenants, runs Right to Rent checks, and sets up the contracts. Once the tenant moves in, you take over.

It's often the best of both worlds: professional marketing and screening, without paying ongoing management fees.

This is the route I've always taken. It suits me perfectly. A gentle arm around me, but I stay in charge. If something goes wrong, I know about it immediately and not after the agent's coffee break.

I prefer working with local agents to the property as this way I can easily drop off keys or any necessary paperwork, and have a face-to-face chat. It's also convenient for tenants signing forms or collecting keys. Plus, there's the added advantage of them advertising your property in their window front.

You can use large chains or smaller local agencies. Large chains offer structure and accountability but have sales targets. Smaller ones can be more personal but harder to reach.

Read reviews (perhaps with a pinch of salt), ask other local landlords, and trust your gut. You can even use more than one agent. Whoever finds the best tenant first, wins. I have nothing against using an online letting agency, but for me, local is my preference.

Best for: New landlords who want help finding tenants but prefer managing their own property.

3. Rent Collection Service

This is when the agent finds the tenant (Tenant-find option), but also collects the rent and manages any arrears. You remain responsible for property maintenance and day-to-day management.

Best for: Landlords who want help with rent collection and arrears, but prefer to manage the property and tenant relationships themselves.

4. DIY (Do it yourself)

You advertise, handle viewings, run credit checks, draft contracts, and collect the rent yourself.

It can feel overwhelming at first, but it's completely doable if you're organised and willing to learn. Plus, it saves you thousands over time. I have heard of landlords using websites such as www.openrent.co.uk, but to date I have never used it and therefore have no experience to share.

Best for: Confident, hands-on landlords who want full control and don't mind a bit of hard graft. **Note:** Under the Renters' Rights Act, please ensure you use an assured periodic tenancy (ASP) template, not an assured shorthold tenancy (AST) agreement.

Managing yourself vs. using an agent

If you're organised, local, and not afraid to get your hands dirty (sometimes literally), self-managing can save you a lot of money.

Letting agents typically charge a monthly percentage of rent for management, or you can pay a one-off 'tenant find' fee. Even if you only use them for tenant sourcing, build a good relationship. It can really help. Remember to add the VAT on top of their quote if they don't mention that to you.

Personally, I avoid full management services. I like to know what's going on, and be available 24/7(ish). I've dealt with burst pipes, broken sinks, toilets and showers, and a boiler breakdown in the height of winter. Because, for me personally, being hands-on means I can take immediate action.

Against some letting agents' advice, I rarely put up rent annually because the risk of the tenants leaving (and the repainting, new carpets, and deep cleaning that follows) often outweighs the extra income. It's nice to be nice and not greedy.

Small vs. large agencies

Small, independent agencies can be personal and flexible, but from my experience, sometimes hard to contact. They may have fewer staff, and this can impact me as a Landlord, and a potential tenant. On the flip side, smaller firms can give a more bespoke service. Ultimately, I want someone who's going to answer the phone to a potential tenant or me, as a landlord.

Large chains tend to have systems, targets, and accountability, but also more 'sales spin' and occasionally less of the personal touch.

Note:

Letting agents promise "peace of mind" for a monthly fee, but sometimes it's just a very expensive forwarding of complaints. Do your research and make your own informed choice.

Top Tip: Choosing an agent

Ask other local landlords, check out their website and trust your gut when speaking to them. You can even list with multiple agents at once, usually at no extra cost. I did that for several years at the start of my landlording journey, as it gave me reassurance that I wasn't putting all my eggs and trust in just one agency I knew nothing about. I chose a small, independent firm, alongside a large chain. Agencies have different people already on their books, so it may help you find the right tenant sooner. And negotiate the fee.

Contracts and deposits

Always use a written tenancy agreement. No handshake deals, no oral agreements are permitted. With the Renters' Rights Act now in place, tenants benefit from a 12-month protected period at the start of a tenancy, during which landlords cannot evict them in order to sell the property or move in themselves. Thus, "no fault" evictions have been abolished. Getting the paperwork right from day one protects everyone – especially you. Currently, a Renters' Rights Act Information Sheet should be given to tenants and can be downloaded from the government website. Check whether your letting agent will be supplying this, if you are using one.

Deposits must be protected in a government-backed scheme. To date, I undertake this task myself and use *mydeposits* so I stay in control. You simply ask the agent to forward the deposit for you, providing you can show it will be protected in a government-backed protection scheme. It saves you money and, in my opinion, potential future hassle. But, for a small fee, agents can hold the deposit on your behalf. You can also ask the letting agent to place it in a custodial account in your name, so you don't have to rely on the agent to return it at the end of the tenancy.

In England and Wales, you (or the letting agent) currently have 30 days to log the tenants' deposit, and at the time of publishing this book, the amount is up to 5 weeks' rent. (However, if the annual rent is £50k or more, the cap is up to 6 weeks' rent). Rules do change, so check with the NRLA or the government website. Some tenants may instead opt for a zero-deposit scheme, where no cash deposit is paid upfront, and the landlord receives protection via a third party. The tenant pays for such protection, and this is usually arranged through the letting agent.

And remember: When a tenant leaves, you can't just keep their deposit because rent wasn't paid – there's a legal process for that.

Hidden extras agents don't shout about

- **Safety checks:** Some agents charge extra for checking your smoke alarm(s) and carbon monoxide alarm(s) are in good working order at the start of the tenancy. I personally check alarms myself beforehand and again on move-in day. Record it on video, perhaps bring a witness, doing so in front of the new tenant(s), if possible.

- **Check-in (and check-out) Inventory:** Often, these are subcontracted to a company that specialises in inventories. While they can be costly, they provide valuable peace of mind. I have occasionally completed inventories myself; however, it is important to be cautious. A self-prepared inventory may carry less weight in the event of a dispute, so it's essential to include clear, detailed descriptions and comprehensive, timestamped photographs to ensure it is robust and reliable.

- **Rent insurance *(optional)*:** Marketed as peace of mind. Personally, I've never used it. Other landlords say payouts aren't as smooth as advertised. Make your own personal, informed decision.

- **Admin charges:** Always ask for a breakdown of fees before signing anything. Remember the 20% VAT!

Do your research

Before you let out your property, spend time on Rightmove or Zoopla. Tick the 'Include Let Agreed' box so you can see what's been rented recently, as well as what's up for rent at the moment.

This helps you gauge:

- What similar properties rent for.
- How much competition there is.
- Whether your price feels realistic.

Personally, I'm not greedy. I'm guided by my agent (they want the best price too), but I have often listed my properties around £50-£100 below market rate.

Why? Because slightly cheaper rent attracts long-term, appreciative tenants. In my experience, that stability is worth far more than chasing every extra pound.

Building relationships with tenants

Whether you self-manage or go through an agent, the real key to success is trust.

Be approachable but not intrusive. Respond quickly to problems.

Be fair with rent increases; keeping a good tenant is often more profitable than turnover. More about this in Chapter 11.

Quick checklist

- ☐ Decide: fully managed, tenant-find, or DIY.
- ☐ Compare agents' fees and services.
- ☐ Question every 'extra' charge with the letting agent.
- ☐ Negotiate your tenancy find fee.
- ☐ Ask to see any potential tenant's reference report.
- ☐ Always use a written contract.

- ☐ Protect deposits in a legal scheme.
- ☐ Don't mix business with friendships.
- ☐ Video the property on move-in day (even if you've paid for an inventory to be undertaken).
- ☐ Build trust from Day 1.

Key Takeaway:

Estate agents aren't all villains, they really aren't. But, from my experience, they're not all heroes either. They have targets and are emotionally detached. See them as a **tool in your toolkit**. Use them wisely, stay in control, and remember:

No one will ever care about your property as much as you do.

CHAPTER 3

Finding the 'Right' Tenant

Even after all these years, the voice of a wise and funny landlady still rings in my ears:

"What you want is a man who is career-focused, no children, works long hours, showers at the gym, spends every weekend at his girlfriend's, gets his shirts dry-cleaned, and has his mum deliver meals on wheels before collecting his washing."

Sounds absolutely fabulous, doesn't it? And while we're at it, I'd like to add a self-cleaning oven and a bin that takes itself out to the list.

Unsurprisingly, Mr Ideal Tenant never showed up. But, hand on heart, despite meeting plenty of *characters* – some lovely, some questionable – I have had (and continue to have) some outstandingly kind and wonderful tenants.

So don't be disheartened. For sure, you will meet a full cast of characters you never auditioned for. But the right one *is* out there. Be patient, trust your gut, and don't ignore those tiny alarm bells your brain starts ringing during viewings.

Pro Tip: Watch for Body Language

People reveal far more with their posture, their fidgeting, and their eye-contact (or lack thereof) than with anything they actually say.

A very experienced landlady once told me, "In a recession, people will always need somewhere to live." And she's right. But that doesn't mean you accept the first person who darkens your doorway, nor does it mean you wait so long that your property starts developing its own personality.

Choose wisely. Move quickly. And remember: you're not looking for perfection. You're just looking for someone who's a decent, respectful human being, who can pay their rent on time, and won't leave salsa stains on the ceiling!

The letting agent's greatest illusion: *The 'ideal tenant'*

I have worked for both an estate and a letting agency, albeit decades ago. From my professional experience, from both sides of the coin, I'm fully aware that letting agents love to present Mr and Mrs Perfect on paper. They have a stable job, great income, no pets, no kids and no drama.

But here's the truth: tenants can (and will) say almost anything to get approved. Things to consider when meeting them:

- Were they on time, and if not, why not?

- Are they over-confident, pushy, or polite and well-mannered – did they offer to take their shoes off?

- Would you be fine having them as your neighbour?

- Do they ask to make immediate changes to the property, i.e. put up partition walls – it does happen!

- How do they speak to their partner or children (if there are any present) when viewing the property?

- Are they clean and presentable?

A good reference matters, but so does tone, consistency, and how people behave during viewings and follow-up conversations. Try to listen for what isn't being said. But also don't be afraid to ask them:

- Where do you currently live? For how long? What about previously?

- Have you rented before?

- Why are you interested in the property/wishing to move?

- Do you know the area?
- Do you have any friends/family nearby?
- Where do you currently work? Can you afford the rent?
- Are you aware of the transport links and the time it will take you to get to work?
- What move-in date do you have in mind?
- How long are you intending to rent the property?
- Do you have any children or family who will also stay here?
- Do you have any pets? If so, how long will they be left alone? (Note: I will speak about pets later in this chapter.)
- Do you smoke?
- Do you have any CCJs (County Court Judgements)?
- Do you have any questions?

The Guarantor

A guarantor is someone – often a parent or close relative – who legally agrees to cover the tenant's rent if the tenant can't pay. Sometimes it's essential, especially if the tenant doesn't earn enough to meet the rent on their own. Guarantors are also helpful for students, first-time renters, or anyone with a limited credit history. Always get a signed agreement and check that the guarantor truly has the means to pay – a promise on paper is only as good as the person behind it. Think of it as a little extra insurance for your sanity and your bank balance.

Top tenant potential red flags

It's hard not to pre-judge others, but when meeting potential tenants, I would recommend acting as though you are interviewing them for a job, because technically, you will be working together during the tenancy agreement, if only on occasion. I would pause before rushing into saying yes to someone who:

"Works in the creative industries" → Are they freelance and do they actually earn a regular wage, enough to pay their rent?

"Can move in tomorrow!" → Why so free? Why so fast? Why so... homeless?

"Offers to pay more!" → Why the urgency? Why so desperate? **Note:** Rental bidding is banned under the Renters' Rights Act, so always stick to the advertised rent.

And if your agent says, "They seemed lovely and polite," that may be true. But remember, so did Ted Bundy.

So yes, agents will hand you glossy profiles and reassuring smiles, but please don't easily be fooled. Your job isn't to find the 'perfect' tenant. It's to find the *right* tenant for *your* property. Someone reliable, respectful, and someone who pays the rent on time!

And that starts with trusting your instincts, asking the right questions, and spotting the red flags your agent 'mysteriously' overlooks.

Protecting your property – and yourself

I'm not suggesting CCTV surveillance, but a quick online search can tell you a lot about a potential tenant.

Ask yourself:

- Do these people behave in the manner projected to you?

Take a quick look at their social media. It can reveal more than an application form ever will. If they claim to be a non-smoker but are happily puffing away on camera, or insist they've no pets while posting cat selfies, that's worth noting. Likewise, watch for any language or behaviour that doesn't align with the standards you'd expect in your property. And if they mention a "small, well-behaved dog", double-check that "small" isn't a Great Dane called Thor. And talking of pets...

How to deal with the new pet rules

Thanks to the new legislation, landlords can no longer simply say "no pets" and move on with their day. Instead, tenants now have the right to ask – and you have the joy of responding reasonably. (Note: I love animals and have many tenants with pets, so I am coming from a non-prejudiced perspective.)

With this in mind:

1. **Be clear before anyone gets emotionally attached.**

   While blanket bans are out, common sense is still very much in. Be upfront about the type of property you're offering and what's realistically suitable. For example, a small, carpeted flat with no outdoor space may not be conducive for every animal – and stating that early can save everyone time, emails and passive-aggressive follow-ups.

2. **Ask Questions (you are allowed to).**

When a tenant requests to keep a pet, you are entitled to information. This is not you being awkward, but you being sensible. Ask them about:

- The type and size of the pet.
- How long they've had it.
- Whether it's house-trained.
- How long it's left for.
- How it's exercised.
- Any references from previous landlords.

3. **Put everything in writing (future you will thank you).**

You will usually have 28 days to respond, and that response should be in writing. Keep it polite and factual. If you say yes, confirm it clearly. If you say no, explain why in property-based terms. Please avoid anything that sounds personal or emotional.

Note: If you are using an agency, email them directly, and if the tenancy is in situ, straight to the tenant – unless the agency is managing it for you.

4. **Decide based on the property, not your past trauma.**

The law expects decisions to be linked to the property itself – size, layout, legal restrictions – not the memory of a Labrador that once redecorated your hallway with its teeth. And note, you don't have to love the idea of pets. You just have to be able to explain your decision calmly and sensibly.

5. **Use the tenancy agreement properly (not vaguely).**

If a pet is agreed, ensure the tenancy agreement clearly reflects it. This is where expectations are set around:

- Damage.

- Cleaning.
- Noise.
- End-of-tenancy agreement.

Hope is not a strategy. Paperwork is.

6. Keep it calm, even if you're internally screaming.

I have been down this road. Many times. Please be mindful that, for tenants, pets are emotional. For landlords, pets are a risk calculation.

Staying calm, consistent, and reasonable doesn't mean you're a pushover – it means you're far less likely to end up arguing about "what was agreed" 6 months down the line.

7. Reasonable doesn't mean reckless.

Allowing a pet doesn't mean accepting unlimited damage, chaos, or surprises. It means approaching requests with a process rather than a knee-jerking reaction.

Handled well, pet requests don't have to be a nightmare. Mismanage them, and they end up as stories landlords laugh about later...eventually.

As a final note, never assume a tenant will manage a pet exactly as you would. For example, pets may be let into the garden rather than walked, animals may not be crated or supervised as promised, and cleaning standards can vary.

Case Study:

One real case I encountered involved a property that looked clean upon departure. However, during the reletting process, the letting agent reported seeing a flea and refused to carry out a viewing due to health and hygiene concerns. The property required professional treatment before it could be marketed again, resulting in delays and unexpected costs.

Lesson: Never rely on assumptions when it comes to pets. Clear written expectations, occasional inspections, and end-of-tenancy checks can help avoid small issues becoming bigger ones.

Should you meet the tenant?

This one divides landlords like pineapple on pizza. And many years ago, I owned a property in a non-desirable area, with huge difficulty parking, and entrusted the agents to find me the ideal tenant, which they did. And rather than have the courage to meet them in person, I had a brief chat over the phone. But that was years ago, when I was young, anxious and mentally exhausted. Today, in my honest opinion, I would say, "ABSOLUTELY YES!" Meeting them, even briefly, helps you gauge their:

- **Vibe** – chaotic or chill?
- **Communication style** – clear or cryptic?
- **Energy** – "reliable tenant" or "carpet destroyer"?

Most people are nice, but you want the right people for your property. So, just remember this isn't about friendship choices. It's:

- Charm versus reliability.
- Tedious versus trouble-free.

- And anyone overly friendly might be hiding something behind that smile and strong perfume.

Because, in truth, what agents tell you and what prospective tenants tell you isn't always the same.

Case In Point:

I once was told that a single young professional wanted to move into my property. Before saying yes, I requested meeting him in person. After chatting, it turned out he was unemployed, had a very young girlfriend who was pregnant and planned on moving in with him. As nice as he seemed, he openly admitted to smoking cannabis, and they were currently living in the grandad's garage, had never paid rent or lived outside of a family home before. This wasn't what the agent told me. Crossed wires? Marketing ploy? I'm not sure. But, at the end of the day, I needed someone who I knew could afford the rent. And, without prejudice, he didn't build my confidence.

Ghost tenants and phantom flatmates

Here's a fun surprise: the person you sign up with might not be the only one living there.

You could end up with:

- Cousins 'just visiting' for three months.
- A rotating cast of mystery boyfriends.
- A casual Airbnb side hustle.

Set clear terms in your tenancy agreement and check in from time to time. Be authentic and ask them to simply let you know if anyone else wishes to move into the property. Left unchecked, your cosy two-bed can quickly turn into a party flat, a long-term storage unit, or a revolving door of strangers.

Being local helps

If you live near your property, you'll sleep more easily. You can pop over for emergencies, fix small issues before they grow, and generally keep an eye on things.

From personal experience, sometimes, it's wise to take someone with you for safety, support and witness. Not to mention being tall enough to reach a smoke alarm, if you don't have a chair or ladder to test it.

Case Study: The Airport Dash

During the pandemic, a tenant called late at night from an airport abroad. He'd reached check-in and realised he didn't have a copy of some necessary visa related paperwork. Boarding was in 30 minutes.

He needed someone to access the property, retrieve the document, and email it immediately.

→

Stressful? Yes.

Doable? Only because I was local.

I got in, found the paperwork, sent it over – and he made his flight. The gratitude was huge.

This is one of the underrated advantages of managing property near where you live. You can respond quickly. You can solve problems in real time. And occasionally, you can save someone from missing an international flight.

Being local doesn't just protect your investment.

Sometimes, it rescues the day.

The rare gems

Every so often, you'll find a tenant who's:

- Respectful.

- Quiet.
- Punctual with rent.
- Genuinely cares about making the property a home.

These people are unicorns. And they do exist. Treasure them, and they'll respect you for it. And not go into an overdrive of emotions if your builder won't be able to fix a wobbly fence immediately. And talking of builders, one way to reduce costs is by using a builder who isn't VAT registered, as they won't charge the additional 20% VAT on labour and services. It's important to note, as with any builder, to make sure they are reputable, properly insured, and suitable for the size of the job.

TLDR

Perfect tenants do exist, but you'll need to vet and filter. Meet them in person where possible. Occasionally, I have gambled on people I liked after meeting them; they appeared honest about their history and circumstances and it paid off, but I wouldn't necessarily recommend taking too many chances.

Bring someone else whose judgment you trust when meeting and interviewing them for the first time. Look them up on social media for validation.

Make notes (it's so easy to forget).

The more red flags you spot early, the fewer excuses, high maintenance tenant and damage due to lifestyle you will face later.

Fraud Protection

Protecting your property from fraud is an important part of being a landlord. Be cautious of scams such as fake tenants, identity fraud, or criminals attempting to sell or rent out your property without your knowledge. Always ensure you or your letting agency carries out thorough references and verifies identities, and keep your details up to date with the HM Land Registry. You can also set up a free Property Alert and consider placing a restriction on your title to help prevent unauthorised transactions. Regular inspections and clear communication can help you spot issues early and safeguard your investment.

CHAPTER 4

Move In and the Welcome Letter

OK, so you've found your perfect – or as perfect as they can be – tenant, signed the papers, and survived the referencing circus. Now it's time for the handover, the moment your tenant officially moves in and your property stops being a project and becomes someone's home.

This stage can either set you up for months of peace or months of pain. Let's make it the first one.

The legal bits

Getting it right from day one.

Before your tenant even crosses the threshold, make sure all the essentials are in place.

Right to Rent Checks

If you are using an agent, they should do this for you, but by law, you must check that every adult tenant has the legal right to rent in the UK. Ask for a valid ID (passport, visa etc.) and keep a copy. If you're using an agent, they'll usually do this. But remember, you are the one who is ultimately responsible.

Keep copies securely filed digitally or on paper, for your records. I do both.

Tenancy Agreements

You must have a written tenancy agreement. Verbal agreements might feel friendly, but they can quickly end in tears – and potentially court fees. You can buy tenancy templates online, or join the National Residential Landlords Association (NRLA) for reliable, up-to-date versions.

With the Renters' Rights Act now in place, these agreements are now known as **Assured Periodic Tenancies (APTs)**, replacing the previous Assured Shorthold Tenancy (AST) agreements. In simple terms, this means the tenancy has no fixed end date and continues until either party gives the correct notice.

If you are using an agent, they will do this for you, but ultimately, your agreement should include:

- Rent amount and payment dates.
- Length of tenancy and notice period (now APTs).
- Responsibilities for repairs and maintenance.
- Rules about pets, smoking, and guests.

Deposits and Protection Schemes

By law, deposits must be protected within 30 days of receipt in a government-approved scheme. This protects both you and the tenant if there's a dispute later.

You have three options:

1. **Let the agent hold it.** It's easier, but you'll pay for the convenience.

2. **Place it in a custodial account.** Either you or your letting agent can do this. In doing so, the letting agent is not involved, and you deal directly with the authorised scheme.

3. **Hold it yourself.** It's cheaper and gives you full control (just make sure you register it properly).

If you're using an agent, they'll usually hold the tenant's deposit, and traditionally it's five weeks' rent (and 6 weeks' rent if the annual cost is £50,000 or more). If you're managing the property yourself, you will need to register the deposit with a government-approved protection scheme such as mydeposits.co.uk or the Deposit Protection Service (DPS).

Here's where it gets a bit tricky: when an agent holds the deposit, you're adding an extra layer between you and your tenant. This can mean:

- You'll pay extra for them to handle it, and don't forget the 20% VAT on top of their fees.

- If there's ever a dispute at the end of the tenancy (say, over cleaning or damage), things can get more complicated, as you'll have to go through the agent rather than dealing directly with the deposit protection scheme.
- Communication can slow down, especially if your agent is managing multiple properties or there's staff turnover.

In short, yes, an agent can save you some admin, but it also adds cost and red tape. Managing the deposit yourself (properly protected, of course) gives you more control and can make resolving issues faster and fairer for everyone.

File all deposit paperwork neatly. Trust me, future you will thank you.

A few extra pointers

- **GDPR:** Collect only necessary tenant data and store securely, use for tenancy purposes only , and respect tenants' rights to access, correct, or delete their information.

- Please make your own informed choice, but I have heard from other landlords that it's probably best not to rely on direct benefit payments if possible. Once those payments stop, recovering rent can be extremely difficult and often involves lengthy delays. However, some landlords prefer them for the security of knowing rent is paid directly from the source. It ultimately depends on your management style and how comfortable you are with potential interruptions or administrative follow-ups.

- Be reasonably flexible with payment dates when needed. For example, if a tenancy begins mid-month and the tenant is paid at the end of the month, you may agree to pro-rata the initial period – provided it does not exceed one full calendar month.

Communication

Find more than one way to reach them.

When your tenant moves in, make sure you obtain **multiple ways to contact them** and not just one mobile number. People lose phones, change jobs, and vanish from WhatsApp faster than you can say, “rent arrears”.

Get:

- A mobile number (and a backup, if possible).
- An email address.
- Their workplace contact (if appropriate).
- An emergency contact (family member or friend).
- It sounds basic, but you’ll thank yourself later if you ever need to track down a vanishing tenant.

The power of a welcome letter

Set the tone early.

Once the legal stuff is sorted and the keys are ready, it’s

time to do something most landlords skip: **Welcome them properly.**

A good welcome letter says, "I'm organised, approachable, and not someone you can take advantage of." It's your first impression in writing. Make it friendly, clear, and quietly firm. Think of it as your landlord handshake.

What to Include:

Keep it simple and practical:

1. **Contact details** – include your phone, email, and what counts as an emergency.
2. **Rent info** – the amount, due date, and payment reference.
3. **Reporting issues** – how and when to report maintenance problems.
4. **Property info** – bin days, stopcock, utility suppliers, meter locations.
5. **Expectations** – a gentle reminder about cleanliness, pets, and guests.

6. **A friendly note** – wish them happiness in their new home. It goes a long way.

Optional bonus: the welcome pack

If you want to make a strong first impression, include a small **welcome pack** with:

- A printed copy of your welcome letter.
- Local takeaways and transport links.
- Appliance manuals (photocopies only – tenants can accidentally and unintentionally misplace these).
- Emergency contacts.
- And maybe even a small gift – biscuits, flowers, or a mini bottle of fizz.

It's a simple gesture that sets you apart as a professional, human landlord and not the villain they've seen in Channel 5 documentaries.

You can find an example of a Welcome Letter, along with a Optional Bonus Welcome Pack at the back of this book.

First impressions matter

When it comes to tenants, remember you're not their friend, but you're also not their enemy. The goal is to be warm but firm, approachable, professional and consistent.

If you start too cold, they'll never call when something's broken. Too soft, and the tenant can become needy and treat you like their personal fixer-upper hotline. If possible:

- Meet them at the property on their move in day.
- Take gas, electricity and water meter readings with them (even if they have already been done). Take photographs if possible.
- Test the smoke and carbon monoxide detector(s) in front of them (even though they would have already been tested). Video, if possible.

- Show them where the stopcock is, how to use it, as well as the fuse board and boiler controls.
- Hand them their keys, labelled accordingly.
- Give them a gentle reminder to use the extractor fan, open windows when possible, and be mindful of condensation and lifestyle that may attribute to mould developing.

Set the tone early, keep it friendly-but-fair, and you'll earn their respect. Offer to arrange an informal check in a week after they move in, if they would like – some issues only become apparent once the tenant has settled in.

Insurance and ongoing requirements

A gentle reminder:

- **Buildings Insurance** – This is essential. It will protect the property, but also you. You can pay monthly or annually, and the more properties you have, the cheaper the individual cost.

- **Smoke Alarms** – One per floor, replaced before expiry.
- **Gas Safety Certificate** – Every year.
- **Carbon Monoxide Alarm** – Diarise the expiry date and your gas safety engineer will advise where best to place it. Have it mounted to the wall.
- **Chimney Sweep** – Annually, if you have a working fireplace. Keep the certificate.
- **Electrical Safety Certificate** – Every 5 years.
- **EPC (Energy Performance Certificate)** – Every 10 years; you might save money by shopping around instead of using the agent's contact.

Tax and record keeping

- Keep detailed records of rent, repairs, mileage, and certificates.

- Consider an accountant and ascertain the software they recommend for your accounts. Depending on your income, as a landlord, you may have to keep digital records and submit updates to HM Revenue and Customs quarterly instead of once a year. I currently use Xero, but there are plenty of other accounting software packages available. The government website, www.gov.uk, has a useful guide to help you choose the right software for making tax digital for income tax, if you do have any doubts.

- Open a separate bank account for all property income/expenses; it will make tax time and rent checks so much easier.

Keep on top of maintenance

- Check in with tenants every 6 months by text, phone or email.

- Take your own meter readings at move-in and move-out. If you are paying for an inventory, the company will do this for you. Personally, I take a quick photo of the readings on my phone on the move-in date, just in case there is a discrepancy, and in case the inventory was done many days prior to the tenant moving in.

- Avoid supplying white goods unless you're happy to clean, repair or replace them.

- Consider boiler cover for older systems.

CHAPTER 5

Pounds, Pennies and Paper Trails

Keeping your finances in check

Being a landlord isn't just about finding tenants and fixing boilers, it's also about managing your money, keeping your paperwork straight, and planning for the long haul. The financial and compliance side of property management might not be glamorous, but it's what separates the calm, confident landlords from the ones losing sleep over tax season.

Separate Bank Account = Sanity Saver

Rule #1: Open a **dedicated bank account** just for your rental income and expenses.

Why:

- Makes it easy to track rent received, repairs, and bills.
- Keeps personal and property finances separate, and this is vital if you're ever audited.
- Simplifies year-end accounting.

Pro Tip:

Choose an online account that lets you export statements directly to your bookkeeping software. Future you will be very grateful.

What to log

Keep clear records of everything that touches your rental property:

- Rent payments (date, amount, method).
- Security deposits received and returned.
- Repairs and maintenance costs.
- Utility bills (if applicable).
- Travel or mileage for property visits.

Keep receipts, invoices, and any email confirmations.

What you can claim

You can claim most expenses that are 'wholly and exclusively' for your property, including:

- Repairs and maintenance (not major improvements).
- Insurance (buildings, contents, and liability).

- Professional fees (accountants, letting agents).
- Travel and mileage related to the property.
- Home office expenses (portion of internet, phone, and electricity if you manage from home).

Tip:

If in doubt, log it. An accountant can always remove something later, but they can't claim what you haven't recorded.

Do it yourself vs. accountant

DIY route:

- Use a spreadsheet or software like Xero, or QuickBooks.
- Cost-effective and great if you're organised.

- Downside: takes time and discipline.

Accountant route:

- Can save you money by spotting deductions you'd miss.
- Handles complex rules and new HMRC updates.
- Varying costs, so shop around for one with property experience.

Middle Ground:

Keep on top of your accounts all year, do the daily bookkeeping yourself, then get an accountant to review before filing. Don't forget, if your earnings require it, quarterly reports are now mandatory, so staying organised pays off.

Tax returns without the tears

Tax returns (self-assessments) aren't fun, but they are absolutely unavoidable. Keep things simple:

- Submit your tax return by 31st January each year for the previous tax year (ending 5th April).
- Keep records for at least seven years. After such time, I sift through and put what's important in a binder in the loft.
- Claim legitimate expenses like agent fees, insurance, maintenance, subscriptions (e.g. NRLA), and replacement of domestic items.

Top Tip: Keep a Paper Trail

I do this partly because if anything happens to me, no one should have to dig through my digital black hole. However, as long as your next of kin can easily access things if needed, and depending on how organised you are, you could scan receipts into a cloud app and finally retire that sad, dusty shoebox of faded paperwork (perhaps putting it somewhere safe, in case of an emergency).

CHAPTER 6

Relationships, Repairs and Retaining your Sanity

Now that the paperwork is signed, the tenant's moved in, the deposit's protected, and everything is filed neatly (because future you is organised now), I don't wish to worry you, but you might think the hard part's over. Spoiler: it isn't.

Once the ink dries, the real work begins. You will be managing people, problems, and the occasional plumbing disaster without losing your sanity (or your Saturday mornings). Welcome to the emotional side of landlording. It's part business, part therapy, and occasionally part comedy show. But trust me, I do sleep at night these days. Here's hoping you will too.

Be approachable, but not a pushover.

There is a fine line between being a nice landlord and a naïve one.

Being approachable means tenants feel comfortable letting you know when something's wrong before it turns into a catastrophe. Being a pushover means you'll be fixing fairy lights at midnight and agreeing to "just one more month" of late rent.

The goal? Strike a balance. Be friendly, professional, and consistent. You can be kind without being a doormat, but for me, that was often easier said than done.

A calm, clear response like:

"Thanks for letting me know. I'll take a look tomorrow."

...is a hundred times better than:

"No problem! I'll be there in five minutes!" (Unless it's a major catastrophe, of course.)

or

"Why didn't you notice this sooner?"

Boundaries + respect = long-term peace for both sides.

Because, as lovely as they are, some tenants are needy, and I learnt this the hard way.

Professional empathy vs. co-dependency

Understanding your tenants doesn't mean adopting them. Professional empathy is listening, caring, and helping where reasonable. Co-dependency is obsessing over whether your friendly tenant can afford his Netflix this month.

Landlording isn't about being a counsellor, bank, or best friend. It's about managing a mutually respectful business relationship. Be compassionate, but keep receipts and structure. Never let someone's personal crisis become your financial one.

Dos and don’ts (from experience, not Google)

DO:

- Be approachable. A friendly tone builds trust.
- Keep your promises; reliability earns respect.
- Fix small issues quickly; prevention beats repair bills every time.
- Document everything, such as texts, emails, receipts.
- Stay on top of smoke alarms and carbon monoxide alarms. They’re your legal responsibility (and they expire).
- Keep learning. Landlord laws change constantly. Joining the Landlords Association might be worth it for templates, updates and a very useful helpline.

DON’T:

- Rent to very close friends. Business and friendship rarely mix.

- Get greedy – annual rent hikes can drive away good tenants.
- Overreact – things break, people make mistakes, life happens.
- Ignore small issues as they rarely stay small.
- Fall for guilt trips. You're a landlord, not a loan provider.
- Become co-dependent. Helping once is kind; becoming a rent-free therapist isn't.

Tenants' biggest fear

Most tenants secretly worry:

> *"If I tell my landlord about the broken door, will they put the rent up?"*

Some landlords do exactly that. But, ignoring problems costs you more in the long run. A broken hinge today can become a broken door next month. A slow leak becomes damp, rot, and eventually an insurance claim.

Your response should balance empathy with firmness:

> *"Thanks for letting me know. I'll arrange for a repair. This won't affect your rent."*

If your tenant feels safe telling you something's wrong, you'll save yourself time, money, and headaches. Trust breeds honesty, and honesty saves cash.

Maintenance: The never-ending to-do list

Things break. Stuff leaks. Tenants lose keys. It's not personal, it's property. A simple maintenance system saves hours of chaos.

It comes at a cost, but you could consider breakdown cover for your boiler, electrics etc. I have used British Gas Homecare in the past, and found it helpful and stress reducing, as I didn't know a reliable plumber, electrician or handyman at the time.

Quick Tips:

- Check in (by text, phone or arrange a visit) every 6 months. A friendly "everything okay?" can reveal hidden issues.
- Encourage early reporting as tenants often delay to avoid bothering you.
- Document repairs. Keep photos, receipts, messages.
- Have a go-to team. To include a reliable plumber, electrician and handyman.
- **Note:** You must give the tenant 24 hours' written notice if you or your representative wishes to enter the property, and the visit must take place at a reasonable time of day.

When helping turns into a habit

Early on, I was too eager to help. I worried a lot. As a result, some tenants thought I had a cape.

- Bird stuck down chimney → rushed over, bird gone.
- Same tenant → mice, with food everywhere → paid for pest control anyway, even though their lifestyle and behaviour were the cause.
- Maggots & dead squirrel → late-night call, rushed over, most issues could have waited.

Lesson: Kindness does not have to equate to 24/7 availability. Assess the urgency before acting upon, and set expectations clearly.

Emergencies & boundaries

Separate true emergencies from drama.

Real Emergencies:

- Gas leaks (evacuate tenants, call emergency line).
- Burst pipes/major leaks.
- No heating/hot water in winter.
- Electrical sparks.

Non-Emergencies:

- Lightbulbs.
- Weird energy in spare room.
- Netflix issues.

Script for Calm:

"Thanks for letting me know. I'll arrange someone first thing in the morning."

Insurance, certificates and staying legal

Another gentle reminder

Keep your paperwork in order:

- Buildings (and contents, if required) insurance.
- Gas Safety Certificate – annual.
- Electrical Safety Certificate (EICR) - every 5 years.
- Smoke Alarms and Carbon Monoxide Alarms - test annually.
- EPC - every 10 years.
- Deposit Protection Scheme (DPS) Certificate – you are legally required to protect the tenant's deposit and provide them with the relevant prescribed information. If you are managing the deposit yourself (rather than through a letting agent), you must ensure the details are correctly logged at the start of the tenancy. The deposit record should then be reviewed and again when the tenant leaves the property.

- Chimney sweep certificate (annually if the fire is in use).
- Any other important documents.

Keep a physical and/or digital paper trail; it's your safety net.

Setting maintenance boundaries

Some tenants expect you to fix everything.

You, the Landlord, are responsible for:

- **Safety:** Gas check, smoke and carbon monoxide alarms, fire-safe furniture, assess for Legionella.
- **Structure:** Walls, floors, ceilings, doors, windows and roof in good repair.
- **Utilities:** Plumbing, electrics, heating, hot water functioning safely.

- **Repairs:** Fix urgent issues promptly; maintain property throughout tenancy.
- **Compliance:** EPC provided; deposit protected in an approved scheme.

Tenants are responsible for:

- Replacing lightbulbs and batteries.
- Keeping the inside and out clean.
- Ventilating the property to prevent mould and damp issues by using extractor fans, opening windows, and wiping any condensation from windows.
- Disposing of rubbish.
- Unblocking sinks, showers and baths (if clogged by hair).
- Maintaining the garden (if there is one).

- Preventing blockages by not flushing nappies, wet wipes or sanitary products down the toilet(s).

Make this clear from the start if you choose to, but remember you're a landlord, not a live-in caretaker.

Proactive maintenance saves £££

Think dental care: ignore it, pay more later.

- £80 boiler service beats £1,200 replacement.
- £70 gutter clean beats £500 ceiling repair.

Perhaps book one maintenance day per year per property. Check seals, gutters and alarms. You will sleep better and hopefully spend less.

Emotional emergencies

Some 'emergencies' are emotional: breakups, lost jobs, stress. Stay calm, stay factual, don't get dragged in.

"I completely understand this is stressful. Let's look at practical steps we can take."

Firm empathy works wonders.

Sanity Saving Tips:

- Keep a spare key – neatly labelled and stored somewhere safe and easily accessible.
- Maintain digital and physical property folders.
- Set office hours (easier said than done). I try not to be on call 24/7, unless in case of an emergency, and I inform the tenants when I go on holiday.
- Celebrate small wins (a month without drama!).

Landlording = patience + paperwork + problem-solving. Calm landlords treat it like a business, not a battle.

TLDR

- Be friendly, not fragile.
- Fix small problems early.
- Stay professional, even when emotions run high.
- Set boundaries early - kindness ≠ chaos.
- Be fair as long-term trust pays off.
- Maintain, inspect, document.
- Protect your sanity. Wine optional, after hours.

Landlording isn't about power. You provide a safe, well-maintained home, and the tenant(s) provide income and care for your investment. Keep that balance, and you won't just keep your sanity, you might even enjoy being a landlord.

CHAPTER 7

Collections and Inspections: Keeping Calm When Things Get Complicated

Collecting rent should be simple: you provide a home, they pay a sum of money, everyone's happy. Reality? Not so much.

Most tenants are prompt, polite, and professional. Others may test your patience, creativity, and tolerance for passive-aggressive texts.

Make rent simple (for both of you)

1. **Set clear expectations at move-in:**

    - Due date.
    - Method of payment.
    - Late Fee Policy: I'm fairly relaxed about this, as I understand that not everyone gets paid exactly when their rent is due. You can also pro-rata the rent to a date that works best for both you and the tenant. Make your own informed choice on this, and refer to the tenancy agreement.

2. **Use online payments:**

    - Standing orders, direct debits, bank transfers. Make it trackable online.
    - Avoid cash; it disappears mysteriously.

3. **Confirm receipt:**

    - A quick text or email (I only do this when the tenant tells me they have paid; most don't): "Rent received with thanks."

- A simple acknowledgement reinforces the habit of paying on time, and this is especially useful for those tenants who have a tendency to pay a few days late.

Handling late payments

Everyone can slip up once in a while, and the occasional late rent isn't the end of the world.

Steps to follow:

1. **Friendly reminder:**

   "Hi [Tenant Name], I noticed this month's rent hasn't arrived yet. Please let me know when you expect to pay."

2. **Formal reminder:**

   If no response, issue a polite, written reminder referencing the tenancy agreement.

   Keep it professional, not threatening.

3. **Escalate if necessary:**

If late payment becomes a recurring issue rather than a one-off, and cannot be resolved, it's important to move from informal reminders to formal action. Under current legislation, this requires relying on a valid ground for possession rather than a no-fault approach, the latter having now been abolished.

If rent is consistently late or unpaid, landlords may rely on rent arrears grounds to seek possession. As legislation can change and grounds vary depending on the circumstances, this is a general guide only – always check official guidance or seek advice from organisations such as the National Residential Landlords Association (NRLA) or the government website to ensure accuracy.

Important Advice:

Do not visit the property in hope to speak to the tenant without formal and prior arrangement. Sometimes – not always – the tenant will better explain their situation in person. You can then explain yours and calmly come to an agreement. The key is not to let emotions run.

Ensure you can cover any expenses if the tenant doesn't pay, to include potential court costs. You might consider a rent guarantee insurance, but this can be costly. Please make your own informed choice.

Keep records like a pro

Document:

- Payment dates.

- Outstanding amounts.
- Texts, emails and letters.

Why? Because if you ever need to take formal action, clear records are your best friend.

> **Tip:**
>
> In the past I have created a simple spreadsheet with columns for due date, paid date, method, and outstanding balance, which I have sent to my late paying tenant as a gentle reminder. This makes it easy to reference and hard to argue with.

When to worry

Red flags for potential rent problems:

- Repeated late payments.
- Vague excuses ("My bank is slow").

- No communication when asked about payments.
- Lifestyle spending that doesn't match income.

If you notice these, address them early. Because waiting usually makes things worse.

When things don't go to plan

Even with the best intentions (and references that looked perfect on paper), not every tenancy runs smoothly. Tenants don't always behave as hoped, and it's part of the reality of being a landlord. Rent may be late, communication can break down, or the property might not be looked after as you'd expect.

The key is not to panic or take things personally. Address issues early, keep communication calm and clear, and give the tenant the opportunity to put things right. If problems persist, don't ignore them. Keep a record of everything and begin to take a more structured approach.

In some cases, you may need to consider ending the tenancy. This should always be a last resort and must be done by following the correct legal process. You'll need to rely on a valid ground for possession and serve the appropriate notice. Avoid acting informally or making arrangements outside the legal framework, as this can cause delays or complications later.

Being a landlord isn't about avoiding problems altogether; it's about how you handle them when they arise. Stay professional, stay consistent, and know when to move from informal conversations to formal action.

Balancing firmness and empathy

Some tenants genuinely hit a rough patch, perhaps a job loss, illness or family issues.

Example: 'Martin' called to explain he'd be a week late paying his rent due to a change of job. I totally understood, adjusted the payment date, documented the plan, and he paid on time thereafter.

Being fair builds trust, reduces stress, and usually means tenants stay longer.

But don't confuse empathy with weakness. Repeated late payments or excuses need formal action as fairness has limits.

Keeping your sanity

- **Separate business and emotion:** Rent is income, not charity.
- **Set boundaries:** No after-midnight texts, unless it's an emergency.
- **Stay consistent:** Treat everyone the same to avoid perceived favourites.

And if you're good with technology:

- **Automate reminders:** Saves time and avoids confrontation.

A calm landlord is a respected landlord. Panic and frustration are contagious. And expensive.

TLDR

- Set clear payment expectations upfront.
- Use online payments and confirm receipt.
- Document everything.
- Address late payments promptly but professionally.
- Balance empathy with firmness.
- Automate where possible; your future self will thank you.

Rent collection doesn't have to be stressful. With clear systems, patience, and boundaries, you can keep the cash flowing and your sanity intact.

CHAPTER 8

Handling Disputes, Complaints and Avoiding Drama

No matter how great a landlord you are, disputes will happen. Tenants are human. You're human. And humans... sometimes complain. Loudly. Frequently. And about things you didn't even know could go wrong.

The goal? Resolve issues professionally, legally, and without unnecessary stress.

Common complaints you'll hear

- *"The heating isn't hot enough."*

- *"The tap is dripping."*
- *"The neighbour is noisy!"*
- *"I don't like the colour of the hallway paint."*
- *"The water pressure is low when the washing machine is on and I want a shower."*
- *"There's mould on the wall!"*

Some complaints are minor, others are out of your control, some are purely dramatic, and some, like mould, are serious and require prompt attention. Your job here is to sort the fact from the fiction and tackle the urgent issues before they escalate.

Mould: Lifestyle and prevention

Mould isn't just unsightly; it's a landlord's worst nightmare. It usually appears when moisture meets poor ventilation, and unfortunately, tenant habits can make it worse. The indoor drying of clothes, with windows permanently shut, or if the tenant is anything like my sons who spend far too long in the shower, the bathroom can easily be turned into a steam room. Combine that with a cold property in winter, and you've got the perfect breeding ground.

How to spot it early:

- Black or green patches on walls or ceilings.
- Musty odours in bathrooms, kitchens, or behind wardrobes.
- Condensation gathering on windows regularly.

Simple prevention tips:

- Keep the property well-ventilated by reminding the tenant(s) to wipe down any condensation on windows daily, open them whenever possible, and use extractor fans. You may consider adjusting the length of time the extractor fan works, or upgrading it.

- Advise tenants to avoid drying laundry indoors. You could provide a drying rack in a ventilated area.
- Encourage tenants to keep heating on at a low level during winter.
- Provide a small dehumidifier if the property tends to feel slightly cold or damp. If damp is persistent or a concern, call in a specialist to assess it properly.

Quick action saves headaches:

If mould appears – and I do advise my tenants of this – clean it immediately and ventilate the area. I do also, when necessary, check for underlying damp issues. Ignoring it won't make it go away, and it will cost more in the long run. I have purchased a plug-in dehumidifier for some tenants and had my builder install a PIV (Positive Input Ventilation) system for others, so I know I'm doing all that I can to support their lifestyle.

Pro Tip:

Include mould-prevention guidance in your tenant welcome pack or move-in briefing. I also talk about everyday lifestyle habits that can contribute to mould when meeting prospective tenants. Most tenants appreciate clarity, and it helps protect the property from avoidable damage.

Dispute Resolution

Put yourself in the tenant's shoes before reacting.

DO:

- **Listen first, act second:** Even if you roll your eyes internally, start with: "Thanks for letting me know. Let's look into it."
- **Document everything:** Keep emails, texts, photos, and notes from calls. Good records protect you if disputes escalate.

- **Respond professionally, not emotionally:** Short, factual, polite responses work best.
- **Set realistic expectations:** Explain clearly what you will and won't do. For example: "I'll arrange a plumber this week. I won't repaint the wall neon green, though."

DON'T:

- Don't argue online, as texts and emails are permanent.
- Don't ignore small complaints, as they often snowball.
- Don't let guilt trips influence decisions, as kindness can be interpreted and/or create weakness.
- Don't promise fixes you can't deliver.

Escalation steps

If disputes can't be resolved informally:

- Send a formal letter or email outlining the issue and resolution steps.
- Refer to the tenancy agreement.
- Join the NRLA (National Residential Landlords Association) for advice.
- Consider mediation; professional third parties often save money and time.
- As a last resort, pursue legal action or small claims.

Pro Tip: Avoid Escalating Drama

Think like a referee, not a participant in the drama.

Staying sane during complaints

- Set office hours. No 2 am WhatsApp meltdowns.
- Take a break before responding to avoid emotional replies.
- Keep perspective, as the problem usually isn't personal.
- Celebrating resolutions and even small wins reduces stress.

TLDR

- Listen, document, respond professionally.
- Avoid emotional reactions or promises you can't keep.
- Balance empathy with clear boundaries.
- Escalate methodically. Mediation before litigation.
- Stay calm. Drama spreads fast, but so does professionalism.

Remember: Handling disputes well isn't about being liked. It's about being respected, consistent, and professional.

CHAPTER 9

Renovations, Improvements and When to Spend (or Save)

Renovations are a double-edged sword. Done right, they can increase the rent, attract better tenants, and make you proud. Done wrong, they drain your wallet, cause endless stress, and make you question your life choices.

The key? Weigh and measure the cost vs. reward. Be realistic about your budget and know when "good enough" is actually good enough.

Know what adds value

Unfortunately, not all improvements pay off, so focus on upgrades that:

- **Increase rent or occupancy**: kitchens, bathrooms, fresh paint, decent flooring.
- **Reduce future maintenance**: new boiler, updated wiring, durable windows.
- **Make tenants happy without overspending**: neutral décor, good lighting, functional storage.

Rule of thumb: Invest smartly. There's no need to spend £10k on a designer kitchen when a well-fitted, good-quality option will keep your tenants happy and your property profitable. Focus on durability and function over flash.

Cosmetic vs. structural

Cosmetic:

- Painting, carpets, minor fixtures, smart lighting.
- Often, the cheapest way to make a property feel fresh and modern.

Structural:

- Roof, plumbing, electrical rewiring, and damp treatment.
- Expensive, but necessary for safety, compliance, and long-term value.

Tip:

Don't skimp on structural work as it's far cheaper to fix now than fight insurance claims or angry tenants later.

Budget like a pro

- Always add 10–20% contingency as renovation surprises are inevitable.
- Keep receipts and invoices safe and secure. It's tax and record-keeping gold.
- Prioritise essential fixes first, luxury touches second, if at all.

Example: Boiler replacement > LED bulbs > 'designer' door knobs.

When to DIY and when to hire

Doing things yourself does save money – if you do it right of course - but costs time and energy. The sooner your house is ready to rent, the quicker you will be earning. In my opinion, I would recommend you hire professionals when:

- It's unsafe (electrical, gas, structural).

- It requires a legal certificate (EPC, gas safety, electrical safety).
- You can't guarantee a quality finish.
- You know you will take far longer to complete and the investment in a professional will be returned quickly, once a tenant is in situ.

Warning:

Never compromise safety or compliance to save a few hundred pounds. It's rarely worth it.

Smart upgrades that impress tenants

- Neutral paint – it appeals to more people.
- Durable flooring – it's easy to clean and maintain. If you do opt for carpets (which I often do), dark (and herringbone or speckled) shades

are better as they help to prevent stains from showing.

- Modern kitchen appliances – a small investment, high return.
- Functional storage – this is always undervalued.
- Efficient heating – tenants love lower bills.

Small touches, like a welcome letter or tidy garden, often make a bigger impression than lavish renovations.

Avoid the money traps

- Over-personalising: the tenant wants neutral; you want turquoise walls and shag carpet.
- 'Luxury' upgrades that don't increase rent enough to cover costs.
- Ignoring long-term maintenance in favour of instant aesthetics.

- Replacing working appliances just because they're 'old'.

Timing is everything

- Plan any necessary renovations between tenancies if possible, as there will be less disruption and fewer potential complaints.
- Spread projects out. Don't try to do everything at once unless you have time, money, and stamina.
- Consider your ROI (return on investment): Will this improvement attract tenants faster, justify higher rent, or reduce maintenance costs?

TLDR

- Focus on upgrades that increase value, reduce headaches, and appeal to tenants.
- Prioritise essential, structural, and functional improvements over aesthetic whims.
- Budget wisely – add a contingency and keep records.
- DIY cautiously – it's safety first, certificates mandatory.
- Smart, strategic renovations beat flashy, over-the-top projects every time.

Renovating a property isn't just about making it look good. It's about making it work for you, for your tenant(s), and for the long-term return on your investment.

CHAPTER 10

Dealing with Emergencies and When to Call in the Professionals

Let's be honest: no matter how organised you are, stuff will break. A pipe bursting late at night, a boiler breaking in January, the smoke alarm shrieking for reasons only it understands.

Unfortunately, emergencies are part of the package. The trick is knowing what you can handle yourself, when to call a professional, and how to stay sane while chaos unfolds.

Common landlord emergencies

- Burst or leaking pipes.
- Boiler breakdowns or no hot water.
- Electrical faults or power outages.
- Fire or smoke alarms going off.
- Flooding from rain or tenant accidents.
- Lost keys or lockouts.
- Broken front or rear doors.

The calm landlord mindset

Step one: Don't panic.

Think: "This is a problem, not a catastrophe."

Step two: Assess risk.

- Immediate danger? Call emergency services or a professional now.
- Minor inconvenience? Schedule repairs at the earliest practical time.

Rule: Safety first, speed second, aesthetics last.

When to DIY vs. call a professional

DIY:

- Minor cosmetic fixes (loose cupboard handle, dripping tap that doesn't flood the kitchen).
- Resetting trip switches, changing lightbulbs.
- Moving small furniture to inspect a leak.

Call a professional:

- Gas, electrical, or structural emergencies.

- Serious leaks, flooding, or broken boilers.
- Fire damage, mould, or anything that could violate health and safety laws.

Tip:

When in doubt, call a professional. They may be able to advise you over the phone on how to fix an issue, such as a boiler pressure problem. No matter, one call – and potential callout – can save you thousands in damages or liability.

Keep a list of trusted professionals

Have a ready list for:

- Plumbers.
- Electricians.
- Gas engineers (registered).

- Locksmiths.
- Builders or handy-persons.

Include:

- Name & company.
- Contact numbers (landline & mobile).
- Approximate rates.

Tip:

Local professionals are gold. They respond faster.

Communicating with tenants

- Keep tenants informed, even if it's just: "Hi, the Engineer is arriving between 10–12 noon. Please keep the area clear."
- Be polite but firm, as it's your property, but emergencies aren't personal.

- Document everything, from emails, texts (screenshot them in case of deletion) and photos.

Example: During a burst pipe, photos of the damage, timestamps, and repair invoices protected both the tenant and me when insurance got involved.

Preparing before disaster strikes

- **Emergency fund:** Always set aside cash for urgent repairs.
- **Boiler cover:** Especially for older systems.
- **Spare keys:** Keep one in a secure, accessible place.
- **Tenant guidance:** Include instructions for minor issues in your welcome pack.

Tenants feel calmer, and small problems are often solved before you even need to step in.

Handling multiple emergencies

Sometimes it rains pipes and fires all at once.

- Prioritise: Safety → Functionality → Comfort.
- Delegate: Professionals do their job; you oversee.
- Keep notes: What was done, when, and by whom.

Panic is contagious. If you stay calm, tenants stay calm.

TLDR

- Emergencies happen, so expect them.
- Safety first, minor damage second, aesthetics last.
- DIY for small fixes; professionals for high-risk issues.
- Keep a local contact list for plumbers, electricians, gas engineers, locksmiths, and builders. Are they VAT registered? The extra 20% cost can make a huge difference.
- Communicate clearly with tenants and document everything.
- Stay calm, as chaos is temporary, your reputation isn't.

Being prepared doesn't just fix problems faster; it helps keep things calm for both you and your tenant(s).

CHAPTER 11

Rent Review: When, Why and How

From experience and speaking to other landlords, this is a landlord's internal tug of war and the big question every landlord faces eventually:

"Should I raise the rent or leave it be?"

Rent increases sound simple on paper, but humans live in houses, not spreadsheets. So let's have a chat about the upside of raising rent, the downside, and why I personally don't hike it every single year unless it really makes sense.

The upside of raising the rent

With the Renters' Rights Act 2026 now in place, landlords have the right to increase rent to the market rate, but only once a year (and the tenant may contest this). To increase the rent (serving at least 2 months' notice), the landlord or letting agent must complete Form 4A, which serves as a Section 13 notice. The form is available online from government housing sites or landlord-support organisations. Make sure you use the correct version for your location (England/Wales; Scotland has different rules) and fill in all required fields accurately, including the current rent, proposed new rent, the date the increase will take effect, and the tenancy details. Serve the notice by hand, post, or email if this is allowed under the tenancy agreement. Ensure you, the landlord, or authorised agent, signs the notice and keep a proof of postage or email receipt if delivered online.

Always check the latest legal requirements when completing the notice – laws may update over time. Personally, I contact the tenant by text or phone in the first instance, pre-warning them I will be serving them notice by post (get a receipt of postage) to increase the rent, and I always attach a friendly cover letter.

Please note that a tenant can challenge the increase in rent, if they feel the proposed rent increase is above the market rate.

However, with that in mind, there are many benefits to raising the rent:

- **More income.** Being a landlord can be costly at times. You want to be fair to both yourself and your tenant(s). And a few extra pounds every month doesn't hurt.
- **Keeps up with market rates.** House prices do change. So do builders' wages.
- **Renovation payback.** New boiler? Fresh carpets? You deserve a little financial hug.
- **Inflation exists.** Bread costs more, milk costs more, electricity costs more – rent sometimes needs to follow suit.

The downside of raising the rent

In theory, putting the rent up makes perfect financial sense. In reality? Not always. Here's why I don't automatically reach for the 'annual increase' button:

- **Good tenants are hard to find and keep.** If you already have reliable, respectful tenants who pay on time, treat the property well, and generally cooperate, raising rent risks losing them.

- **Avoiding greed perception.** I don't want to alienate tenants by seeming greedy or exploitative. Keeping rent reasonable shows respect and builds trust.

- **More self-sufficient tenants.** Tenants who pay lower rent often don't feel as pressured to contact me about every small issue. They may fix minor problems themselves (e.g. replacing a small part), saving me time and potential expense.

- **Reduced 'bother factor'.** When rent is lower, tenants might feel less anxious about requesting help – ironically, they might feel more comfortable asking, or less afraid that complaining will trigger a rent rise. This can lead to less friction and smoother landlord-tenant relations.

- **Long-term stability over short-term gain.** A modest rental increase might offer immediate extra income, but losing a good tenant (and facing months of vacancy, lost income, re-letting costs, cleaning/repairs) could outweigh short-term gains.
- **Goodwill & reputation.** A reputation for fairness can attract and retain better tenants in the long run; over time, that stability becomes more valuable than marginal increases.

Final Thoughts About Rent Increases

- Harmony is underrated.
- Sometimes, the best profit a landlord gets is peace of mind. Because raising rent isn't just maths – it's psychology, timing, and compassion.
- Raise rent when it's fair, needed, or long overdue. But remember: A great tenant is worth more than a slightly bigger bank balance.
- If a tenant is respectful, pays on time, and doesn't redecorate the lounge in zebra stripes, I'd rather keep them happy than add £25 and risk a 'For Rent' sign.
- A rent increase should feel justified – not expected. When it's handled thoughtfully, with transparency and fairness, both landlord and tenant benefit in the long run.

CHAPTER 12

Ending Tenancies, Deposits and Saying Goodbye Gracefully

Every tenancy comes to an end. Sometimes it's planned and straightforward. Sometimes it's messy and stressful. And sometimes, it's genuinely sad, because tenants you've built a good relationship with move on, leaving a space that feels unexpectedly empty.

The goal? Leave the property in good shape, get their deposit sorted, and preserve your sanity, preferably in that order.

Notice Periods: Timing is everything

Tenants must always provide the correct notice. And have it put in writing. It's essential to check the government website, as rules do change, but under the Renters' Rights Act, tenancies now move to a periodic structure, and tenants are required to give at least two months' notice when they wish to leave. Always check your tenancy agreement first. If you are on a joint contract, one tenant has the right to give notice without the agreement of the other occupier. In doing so, the tenancy will end for everyone.

Landlords, on the other hand, can no longer simply ask a tenant to leave without a reason. For most grounds, you need to give at least four months' notice. Certain situations, like rent arrears or anti-social behaviour, allow for shorter notice periods. If you need to end a tenancy, you must follow the correct legal process and rely on one of the approved grounds for possession, giving the appropriate notice period for that ground. Check the government website, NRLA or your letting agent, if you use one, for accuracy.

Key Takeaway:

Notice works both ways and getting it wrong can cost you time, money, and a great deal of unnecessary stress. Ensure everything is in writing.

Final inspection

Treat the final inspection as a gentle audit. To support both you and the tenant – and help avoid unnecessary disputes – it can be useful to provide another copy of the inventory around a month before they move out (if they no longer have theirs to hand). This acts as a helpful reminder of any actions they may need to take, such as returning walls to their original colour, cleaning the oven, mowing the lawn, or defrosting the freezer (if provided).

Remember, you're not looking for perfection, you're checking for:

- Damage beyond fair wear and tear.

- Missing items from the inventory.
- Cleanliness (within reason, as you're not expecting Michelin standards).
- If applicable, a neat and tidy garden, free from dog faeces.

Take **photos, videos if possible,** and make **notes**. They're your defence if there's a dispute.

Deposits: Holding, protecting, and returning

Who Held It?

- **Using an agent:** If your letting agent holds the deposit within a government-backed tenancy deposit protection scheme, contact them in the first instance. You may have arranged for the deposit to be placed in a custodial account in your name; if so, you won't need to rely on the agent to release it at the end of the tenancy and can deal directly with the authorised scheme.

- **Self-managing:** If you manage the tenancy yourself, you would have arranged for the agent to forward the deposit to you and then protected it in a government-backed scheme (such as *mydeposits*). Both you and your tenant will hold a deposit protection certificate. At the end of the tenancy, you can log in to the scheme, release the deposit, and return the appropriate amount accordingly.

Note: Some tenants may have used a zero deposit scheme, which they paid for annually. The scheme will cover any monies owed to the landlord on the tenant's behalf.

Never hold it in cash under a mattress, not unless you like sleepless nights worrying about theft, forgetting, or legal trouble.

Returning the Deposit

- Return it promptly if the tenant leaves the property in a reasonable condition. I wouldn't hang about and instead return their deposit to them as soon as you can. Technically, you've got up to 28 days, but if there's no dispute, I say the sooner the better. It's a simple gesture that ends things on good terms and shows you're fair, especially if you're returning the full amount.

- Deduct only for documented damage or unpaid rent.
- Itemise any deductions clearly. A list plus photos saves arguments.

Pro Tip:

If tenants challenge deductions, the deposit scheme will mediate. Your photos and notes are gold.

Cleaning and repairs

- Be firm but fair.
- Minor scuffs, nail holes, or faded paint = tenant responsibility? Usually not.

- Broken items caused by neglect? Deduct fairly.
- Don't overcharge; it may backfire if the tenant disputes.

Case Study:

One tenant painted their son's bedroom a vivid, bright blue without asking. Upon departure, I also noticed the stones from the fireplace were missing. Thankfully, I had clear photos and a solid tenancy agreement, so the deduction process was simple and relatively drama-free. I even offered them the chance to repaint the room back to its original colour, and purchase the stones for a full deposit return, but they declined.

Note: You can't use the tenant's deposit to cover unpaid rent. This is a separate issue that must be pursued through the proper process.

Exit communication

Just like your welcome letter, a short, polite 'goodbye note' sets the tone. You might like to write something like this:

> [Address of property]
>
> [Date]
>
> Dear [Name of Tenant].
>
> Thank you for being a tenant at [Property]. I hope your time here has been comfortable and enjoyable. If there are any final matters to address, such as forwarding on any mail, please let me know. Your deposit will be returned promptly after the inspection.
>
> Wising you all the best.
>
> Kind regards
>
> [name]

Polite, professional, and leaves no room for drama.

Over the years, I've found it pays to be kind whenever you can (unless there's a clear reason not to be). A simple card or small gift can mean a lot and help end the tenancy on a positive note. Some tenants have returned years later, which is always lovely. Of course, it doesn't always work out that way, so use your judgment, stay fair, and approach each situation with a balanced perspective.

Tip:

When a tenant moves out, they often redirect their post, and this can affect important notices that may be meant for you. Make sure you provide your own residential address for correspondence, along with your email address, when contacting energy suppliers and the local council, for example.

Common mistakes to avoid

- **Delaying inspections**. This opens the door for damage disputes.

- **Guessing deductions**. Tenants can challenge you.
- **Getting emotional**. It's a business transaction, not personal.
- **Assuming fairness is obvious**. Document everything.
- **Left-behind items:** If tenants leave belongings after moving out, store any valuable items safely and try to contact the tenant. Give them a reasonable period (commonly 14–28 days) to collect their property before disposing of or removing it. Always keep a record of what was left and how it was handled.

Tenants who leave on good terms:

- Might return next time.
- Might recommend you to friends.
- Won't leave a lingering dispute over their deposit.
- Even if the tenancy ended badly, a professional approach reduces stress and legal risk.

Graceful Exits = Fewer Headaches.

Re-advertising

With the Renters' Rights Act in place, you, as a landlord, are now restricted from re-letting – or even advertising – your property for 12 months after your tenant vacates. In practice, this can mean up to 16 months from the date a Section 8 notice is served. However, if possession is granted on alternative grounds (for example, rent arrears), this restriction does not apply and ends on the date possession is recovered.

Perhaps use this period productively by completing any necessary repairs or improvements, helping to enhance the property's appeal and support your intended rental value.

TLDR

- Know the legal notice periods and follow the tenancy agreement.
- Schedule the final inspection early and document everything.
- Return deposits promptly, deduct fairly, and explain deductions clearly.
- Use polite, professional communication, even when things go sideways.
- Treat the move-out as a **business transaction** and keep emotions in check.

Ending a tenancy well is just as important as starting it well. It's your last chance to leave a professional impression, close the account cleanly, and prevent lingering headaches.

CHAPTER 13

The Rewards – Yes, There Are Some!

Let's be honest: if you're a new landlord, the horror stories probably have you double-checking your locks at night. Facebook groups can be helpful, but also a scaremongering hindrance. But despite the sleepless nights, the broken boilers, and the maggot incidents, being a landlord comes with some very real rewards.

Financial independence

Rental income isn't just money in your pocket; it's freedom:

- Supplement your salary or offset mortgage costs.
- Reinvest profits into additional properties. Never say never again, like I once did.
- Create a passive income stream that doesn't disappear when your day job ends.

The Goal: Make your money work for you, instead of you working for it.

Security for retirement

Owning property gives long-term stability:

- Unlike stocks or pensions, bricks and mortar are tangible assets.
- A well-maintained property can generate income for decades.

- Planning and saving through your rentals can mean a worry-free retirement.

Think of your properties as a nest egg that grows over time.

Stories of good tenants (yes, they do exist)

They're less rare than you think, and they do exist. These are the types of tenants who make all the headaches worthwhile:

- Quiet, responsible, respectful, and timely with rent.
- They treat your property as if it were their own.
- They communicate clearly when something needs attention.

Case in point: I once had a tenant leave me a bunch of flowers, a hand-written thank you card, and a genuinely heartfelt note. It caught me completely off guard and meant more than I can easily explain. It's just one of many small gifts and kindnesses I've experienced over the years, but it stayed with me. Moments like these remind you why you do this. You're not just managing a property – you're helping someone build a life, create memories in a place they can truly call home.

When everything works smoothly

There's nothing quite like the satisfaction of:

- Rent paid on time, every time.
- No unexpected maintenance emergencies.
- Tenants who leave the property in a better condition than they found it.
- Tenants – and sometimes their families – who tell you they appreciate what you have done for them.

It's still worth it

Please make your own informed choice, but even with all the stress, most landlords report that the long-term rewards outweigh the headaches:

- Financial stability and independence.
- Control over your investments.
- The pride of owning property and helping tenants have a safe home.
- Learning invaluable life skills, such as negotiation, problem-solving, and crisis management.

TLDR

There are bad days, but the rewards - financial, personal, and emotional - make it worthwhile.

CHAPTER 14

Tales from Both Sides: Landlord and Tenant Wisdom

Being a landlord is part adventure, part chaos, and part "What did I sign up for?" This chapter collects stories, lessons, and practical tips from landlords – including me – and insights from tenants, so you can survive (and maybe even enjoy) the ride.

Lessons learned stories from landlords

The Shower Screen Fall: A heart-stopping moment as their child was in the bath when the glass screen came crashing down. **Lesson:** Always check fixtures and fittings regularly, especially in bathrooms where children or vulnerable tenants are present. And yes, keep trusted contacts like a plumber on speed dial. Prevention beats panic.

Glitterpocalypse: A tenant decided to cover the living room in sparkly wallpaper without permission. Removing it was a complete nightmare. The same went for stickers plastered across the child's door. **Lesson:** Set clear rules in the tenancy agreement about alterations.

Ghost Tenants & Phantom Flatmates: Cousins, partners, Airbnb guests... surprise inhabitants can appear. **Lesson:** Clarify occupancy in your contract and inspect periodically.

Pest Control – Sometimes You Step In: Being local has its perks, as well as its early-morning horror stories. Take the time a tenant called at 5 am, screaming that maggots were falling from the bathroom's extractor fan. The culprit? A dead squirrel in the loft. Upon arrival, salt was strewn across the lino and landing carpet, the tenant in full panic mode. Sometimes I have had to roll up my sleeves on occasion and other times I have asked a trusted friend or paid for pest control. Check your tenancy agreement too, as it may state that it is the tenant's responsibility. Still, squirrels chew wires and mice multiply fast, so when it comes to pests, it's not glamorous, but handling it quickly calms the tenant, prevents escalation, and stops small problems becoming big – and costly – ones.

Advice from landlords

- **Document everything:** Every repair, payment, and tenant interaction should be recorded. It will save headaches later.
- **Don't mix business and friendship:** Renting to friends or family rarely ends well.
- **Local contractors are gold:** Quick response, reasonable rates, and fewer excuses.
- **Expect the unexpected:** Build buffers into your budget and schedule.

Tips that save time, money and sanity

- **Templates & Checklists:** Welcome letters, inspection checklists, maintenance logs, rent reminders. Automation is your friend.
- **Software for Organisation:** Accounting software and spreadsheets for tenant records.
- **Emergency Fund:** Even a small buffer turns a crisis into a minor inconvenience.
- **Multiple Contact Methods:** Phone, email, WhatsApp and never rely on just one.
- **Act Quickly on Repairs:** Small issues are cheaper to fix early than when they turn into full-blown disasters. Build a list of reliable tradespeople you trust.
- **Positive Tenant Relationships:** Good communication and mutual respect can prevent many problems before they start.

Real-life maintenance and mould stories

The Wardrobe Rant: One tenant called me on Saturday evening, furious about the mould behind their wardrobe. It turned out that their lifestyle was the culprit. They had a baby, and laundry was drying constantly indoors. When they eventually moved out, no mould issues reoccurred. **Lesson:** Sometimes the problem isn't the property; it's how it's used.

Dehumidifier Success: Another tenant struggled with damp. I bought a dehumidifier, and the problem vanished. Small investments can go a long way.

Roof Conundrum: A leak appeared in a property. The builder inspected the issue, repaired the roof, the tenant was satisfied, and further damage was prevented.

Trees & Ventilation: Another property surrounded by trees had poor airflow. The builder installed a PIV (Positive Input Ventilation) system in the loft. Problem solved, tenant ecstatic.

The Hairy Situation: Shortly after a tenant gave birth, a landlord received a frantic call about a leak from the ceiling.

Turns out, an epic tangle of hair had clogged the pipes. Postpartum hair shedding is a real thing, and combined with a new baby's bath times, the pipes simply couldn't cope. **Lesson:** Sometimes plumbing problems aren't about the property; they're about life happening in it. Regular maintenance, drain guards, and a little patience go a long way. And yes, having a trusted plumber on speed dial never hurts!

TLDR

Every complaint isn't a catastrophe. Handle calmly, practically, and promptly. Lifestyle issues, small fixes, and minor investments save stress and money.

Caring about your tenant matters, but please don't let yourself be bullied into dropping everything for a non-urgent repair. Sometimes, the most urgent thing a landlord can do is learn when to say, "It can wait", vs. "I'm on my way!"

What tenants appreciate

Tenants may love the property, but what makes them happy and likely to stay?

Responsiveness: Answer emails, texts, or calls promptly.

Clarity: Be clear about rent, rules, and expectations.

Consistency: Treat all tenants fairly.

Respect: Give notice before visits; respect privacy.

Common tenant peeves

- Ignoring small repairs until they become major headaches.
- Surprise rent increases or hidden charges.
- Disappearing for weeks with no response.
- Micromanaging their day-to-day life.

The small touches matter

Small touches that have a positive impact:

- **Welcome Pack/Letter:** Intro, rules, appliance instructions, bin schedules, local tips.
- **Prompt Repairs:** Shows you care.
- **Check-Ins:** Short messages asking if everything's okay.
- **Occasional Gestures:** A card at Christmas or a small upgrade.

Happy tenants = longer tenancies, fewer void periods, and less stress.

Key Takeaways

- Landlord horror stories are inevitable; that's part of the adventure.
- Learning from mistakes and having systems in place keeps stress manageable.
- Humour helps. If you can laugh at the chaos, you'll survive it.
- Communication and respect are key. Solve problems early.
- Little gestures matter more than you think.
- Being professional, fair, and approachable keeps everyone happy.

Keep calm and landlord on

Landlording isn't perfect. It's messy, unpredictable, and occasionally exhausting. However, with balance, patience, a sense of humour, and a bit of planning, you can turn the chaos into success.

> **TLDR**
>
> Plan, document, communicate, laugh, repeat.
>
> Do this, and your property business won't just survive, it can genuinely thrive.

BONUS CHAPTER

Things to Consider when Buying a Rental Property (and When to Sell)

This chapter exists because my youngest son asked me to add it. He's at the stage of life where buying his first property – possibly as a rental – feels exciting, overwhelming, and full of questions that no one really answers properly. He said he thought this chapter would be really helpful for him.

A quick disclaimer: I'm not a property expert, financial adviser, or guru. What I do have, though, is 20+ years of lived experience, and with my son keen to hear my thoughts, it felt worth sharing – in case it helps other readers too.

When I first started out, I thought buying a rental was mostly about numbers. Yield in, expenses out, job done.

Reality, of course, had other plans.

Over time, I learned that the best rental decisions are rarely just financial. They're practical, emotional, and sometimes about asking yourself uncomfortable questions, like *"Would I feel safe turning up here at 10 pm if something went wrong?"*

Location isn't just about postcodes

For me, it was essential that I felt comfortable visiting the property late at night. That meant thinking about street lighting, parking, and general safety – not just during the day, but in the real world, after dark.

If you dread the thought of popping over in an emergency, that feeling won't improve with time. I have been there, done that.

It's not essential, but being local (or at least easily reachable) makes a significant difference. Quick visits can calm situations, reduce unnecessary escalation, and stop small issues from snowballing. I've known landlords who eventually sold up, worn down by hours spent travelling just to inspect a 'possible issue' or sort a minor repair – all because they avoided full management to save on fees and keep control, only to discover the hidden cost was their own time and sanity.

Beware the 'Charming' Tree

Large, mature trees look lovely in estate agent photos. Insurance companies, however, are far less romantic.

Properties near big trees often come with higher insurance premiums, potential subsidence risk, blocked drains, falling branches, and roots that slowly but enthusiastically go where they shouldn't.

It's not a deal-breaker – but it is something to price in before you fall in love with the view.

Think about yield, but also flexibility

Yield matters. Of course it does. But so does who your property will appeal to when life (or the market) changes.

Two-up, two-down houses are, in my opinion, the unsung heroes of rental property. They're affordable, practical, and attractive to a wide range of people:

- Single professionals.
- Couples.
- First-time buyers.
- Single parents.
- Divorcees starting again.

That broad appeal makes them easier to rent and easier to sell. When the time comes to exit, you're not stuck with a niche property and limited options.

Always buy with one eye on the exit

Even if you plan to hold a property long term, always consider how easy it would be to sell.

Ask yourself:

- Who would buy this if I needed to sell quickly?
- Is it mortgageable for most buyers?
- Would I still want it if interest rates doubled or demand dipped?
- Would I be happy living in the property if I absolutely had to, or want my children to? If the answer is no, I won't buy it.

If those questions make you uncomfortable, it's worth pausing.

First rental property checklist

Before buying a property for rental, my advice would be to tick off the following:

- [ ] I feel safe visiting the property at night.
- [ ] Parking is straightforward and doesn't require a minor miracle.
- [ ] The property appeals to more than one type of tenant.
- [ ] It would also appeal to a future buyer.
- [ ] The rent comfortably covers costs, not just on paper.
- [ ] Insurance costs are reasonable (trees, location, and structure considered).
- [ ] Maintenance feels manageable, not overwhelming.
- [ ] I'm not relying on everything going perfectly for this to work.
- [ ] I can afford a void period without panic.
- [ ] Owning this property supports my life – it doesn't overly complicate it.

If you're hesitating on several points, pause. A good deal will still be a good deal tomorrow.

When to consider selling

Sometimes selling isn't failure – it's experience talking.

You might consider selling if:

- The property causes ongoing stress.
- Maintenance costs are creeping up.
- The yield no longer stacks up.
- Your life circumstances change.
- You simply want your time and energy back.

A rental should support your life, not dominate it.

Buying well makes landlording easier. Buying badly makes every issue heavier than it needs to be.

Closing thoughts

If there's one thing I hope you take from this book, it's this: landlording doesn't have to be loud, stressful, or fuelled by constant urgency.

Most of it is about calm decisions, clear boundaries, and learning when to act – and when not to.

You'll make mistakes. Everyone does. You'll also have moments when you handle something better than you ever expected. Both are part of the process.

The goal isn't perfection or squeezing every last pound out of a property. It's stability. It's fairness. It's being able to sleep at night without dreading the sound of your phone.

Property should support your life, not dominate it.

If this book has helped you feel a little more prepared, a little more confident, or simply less alone in the realities of being a landlord, then it's done what it set out to do.

And finally...

For my two sons and the reader:

May this book support you in your landlording journey. And may your choices bring you stability, confidence, and peace of mind.

BACK SECTION

Templates, Forms and Notes

This section is designed as a **practical companion** to your guide. Keep it handy for jotting down essential details, storing templates, and having all your go-to contacts in one place. Think of it as your mini command centre for smooth, stress-free landlording. Alternatively, use these templates as guides and create your own.

Tip:

Use the next few pages as a running log as the small details often save headaches later.

Sample welcome letter

Dear [Tenant's Name],

Welcome to your new home at [address]. I hope you'll be very happy here.

A few quick notes for ease:

- **Contact:**

  Urgent issues: call/text [number]

  Non-urgent issues: email [email address]

  Alternative contact:

  Name: [name and relationship]

  Call/text: [number]

- **Rent:** £[amount] due on [date] each month. Please use reference [property/address]. Bank details are [insert bank details].

- **Emergency shut-offs:** Stopcock is [location]. Gas/electric meters are in [location]

- **Bins:** [insert collection days & recycling info]

If you have any questions or you have any concerns, please don't hesitate to let me know.

Wishing you all the best settling in.

Warm regards,
[Your Name]

[Your Contact Details]

Optional bonus: The welcome pack

If you want to make a strong first impression, include a small **welcome pack** with:

- A printed copy of your welcome letter.
- Local takeaways and transport links.
- Appliance manuals (photocopies only – tenants can accidentally and unintentionally misplace these).
- Emergency contacts.
- And maybe even a small gift – biscuits, flowers, or a mini bottle of fizz.

Key contacts

Service	Name	Phone	Email	Notes
Plumber				
Electrician				
Handyman				
Gas Engineer				
Accountant				
Insurance Company				
Letting Agent				
Emergency Services				

Inspection checklist – routine property checks

Property Address: ______________________________

Date of Inspection: ______________________________

Inspector: ______________________________

Structural & Safety Checks

- Walls, ceilings, and floors (cracks, damp, damage).
- Doors and windows (locks, hinges, seals).
- Smoke alarms & carbon monoxide alarms (test batteries).
- Gas & electrical appliances visible condition.

Plumbing & Heating

- Taps, sinks, showers (leaks, dripping).
- Toilets & cisterns (flushes properly).
- Boiler & radiators (functioning, leaks).

- Hot water temperature.

Interior & General Condition

- Kitchen – appliances, cupboards, cleanliness.
- Bathroom – tiles, grout, mould.
- Living areas – walls, floors, fixtures.
- Bedrooms – furniture, flooring.

Exterior (if applicable)

- Garden, fences, gates.
- Roof & gutters.
- Driveway, garage, shed.

Notes / Actions Required:

Rent reminder template

Subject: Friendly Reminder – Rent Due

Dear [Tenant Name],

I hope you're well. This is a polite reminder that rent for [Property Address] is due on [Due Date].

Amount Due: £[amount]

Please ensure the payment is made by [Date]. If you've already paid, thank you! If not, please let me know if there's any issue so we can discuss it.

Thank you for your prompt attention.

Best regards,

[Your Name]

[Phone / Email]

After all the horror stories, tips, and advice, it helps to have a central hub of contacts, associations, and tools to keep you sane and compliant.

Landlord Associations

Joining a landlord association gives you access to legal updates, templates, and advice:

- **National Residential Landlords Association (NRLA)** – www.nrla.org.uk. (Formed from the merger of the NLA and RLA, and now the main national body for landlords.)
- **GOV.UK – Private Renting Guidance** – www.gov.uk. This is the source of truth for legislation, rights, responsibilities, and what you can and can't do without landing yourself in trouble.
- **Local landlord forums and Facebook groups** – Great for peer support and local tips.

Tip:

Associations often have templates for tenancy agreements, deposit letters, and inspection checklists.

Compliance and professional contacts

This section is designed to help you stay organised, track key information, and personalise your landlord journey. Use it for everything from contractor contacts to inspection notes.

Pro Tip:

Keep a folder or spreadsheet with contacts, certificates, and expiry dates for each property.

Property and tenant details

Property Address	Tenant Name	Start Date	End Date	Deposit Held

Tip:

Include multiple lines per property for each tenant over time.

Certificates and renewals tracker

Certificate	Issue Date	Expiry Date	Notes
Gas Safety			
Electrical			
EPC			
Smoke/CO Alarms			
Chimney Sweep			

Maintenance and repair log

Date	Issue	Action Taken	Cost	Contractor	Notes

Keep a running log to show patterns and prevent minor issues from escalating.

Recommended reading and video links

Books, podcasts, and videos can save you time and mistakes:

- Books on landlord law, property management, and DIY maintenance.
- YouTube channels and webinars for quick how-to guidance.
- Podcasts with landlord stories, tips, and lessons learned.

Keep a small list of your favourite resources handy. It's like having a mentor on call.

Notes

Here's space for you, perhaps to record:

- Maintenance reminders.
- Ideas for property improvements.
- Lessons learned from tenants.
- Observations from inspections.

Notes:

Notes:

Notes:

Thank you for reading

This book reflects what I've learned over the past 20+ years – the good, the difficult, and the things I wish I'd known earlier.

If you'd like to explore more or see what I'm working on next, you can find me online at **www.lisabentley.co.uk**.

And if you found this book useful, a short Amazon review would be warmly appreciated.

Lisa

Living In Service Always

www.ingramcontent.com/pod-product-compliance
Lightning Source LLC
La Vergne TN
LVHW052321200926
848481LV00002B/626